Unspeakable

New Studies in Theology and Trauma

Series Editors:

Scott Harrower
Preston Hill
Joshua Cockayne
AND
Chelle Stearns

Forthcoming Books in the Series:

Dawn of Sunday: The Trinity and Trauma-Safe Churches
by Joshua Cockayne, Scott Harrower, and Preston Hill

Unspeakable

Preaching and Trauma-Informed Theology

Sarah Travis

FOREWORD BY
Paul Scott Wilson

CASCADE *Books* • Eugene, Oregon

UNSPEAKABLE
Preaching and Trauma-Informed Theology

New Studies in Theology and Trauma

Cascade Books
An Imprint of Wipf and Stock Publishers
199 W. 8th Ave., Suite 3
Eugene, OR 97401

www.wipfandstock.com

PAPERBACK ISBN: 978-1-7252-6797-8
HARDCOVER ISBN: 978-1-7252-6798-5
EBOOK ISBN: 978-1-7252-6799-2

Cataloguing-in-Publication data:

Names: Travis, Sarah, author.

Title: Unspeakable : preaching and trauma-informed theology / by Sarah Travis.

Description: Eugene, OR: Cascade Books, 2021 | New Studies in Theology and Trauma | Includes bibliographical references.

Identifiers: ISBN 978-1-7252-6797-8 (paperback) | ISBN 978-1-7252-6798-5 (hardcover) | ISBN 978-1-7252-6799-2 (ebook)

Subjects: LCSH: Preaching. | Psychic trauma—Religious aspects—Christianity. | Post-traumatic stress disorder—Religious aspects—Christianity. | Theology, Practical.

Classification: BV4335 T73 2021 (print) | BV4335 (ebook)

06/07/21

Contents

New Studies in Theology and Trauma

N ew Studies in Theology and Trauma is a series of entry-level mono-graphs in Christian theology engaging trauma. The series showcases work at the intersection of trauma and theology from emerging scholars in this new discipline. Each volume will be approximately 60,000–80,000 words long according to the topic at hand. Monographs in the series are aimed at exploring: (i) how trauma studies and trauma theory can inform theological method, (ii) how theology can be used as a frame for under-standing trauma, (iii) how churches and faith communities can facilitate theologically informed, effective trauma care.

Recent neuroscience has confirmed that surviving traumatic violence leaves lifelong scars in the brain and body, and that "the body keeps the score." This persistent reality of trauma poses a unique challenge to Chris-tian communities and churches. Thankfully, many of these communities have begun to recognize that trauma and abuse do not happen "out there" but are horrors that occur within our own ranks, with many Christians call-ing out for justice for victims that have hidden in the shadows far too long. Christians cannot avoid confronting trauma that is tragically manifesting within our own church communities. When trauma is perpetrated by pas-tors and Christian leaders, this threatens to undermine a Christian witness to the gospel. As a result, trauma is raising the stakes on theological truth-claims made by Christians. This leaves a door wide open for Christians to explore the intersection of theology and trauma.

Given the emerging state of literature on theology and trauma cur-rently, there is a need to solidify the intuitions shared by scholars in the many disciplines of theology and biblical studies and signal a constructive and generative approach for the future of this growing field. The present series seeks to fill this need by offering a series of monographs grouped around a *double-witness*: a witness to the laments and losses involved in surviving trauma and a witness to God's ongoing presence and agency in the aftermath of violence. By promoting a double-witness approach in this series, authors engaging theology and trauma will be provided a coherent and fruitful platform for witnessing both the wounds of trauma and the healing in recovery for communities today.

We have started this series because trauma calls for faithful and generative witness, which is why we have selected the Australian lyrebird as the symbol for our series. The lyrebird is able to listen carefully to sounds of its surroundings, then repeat these back in concert with new voices as part of a broader song. This new song is unique in that it faithfully reflects the original sounds into a new context of richer harmony. Likewise, empathetic listening that faithfully witnesses the wounds of trauma while remaining open to renewed hope within a larger frame is the core idea of the New Studies in Trauma and Theology Series.

Series Editors:

Scott Harrower, Preston Hill, Joshua Cockayne, and Chelle Stearns

Foreword

I t is hard to think of a more timely volume on preaching than this one dealing with trauma and the gospel. Its publication will be in what are hopefully the final months of the COVID-19 pandemic. The pandemic will end, but it may be many years before the trauma left in its wake is over for many people. We may face a new long-term pandemic of post-traumatic stress.

Sarah Travis speaks of trauma with sensitivity and insight, in vulnerable and informed ways, asking the kinds of questions every preacher is right to ask. How do we preach good news in the face of traumatic events, offering words that are authentic and substantial, not just nice words that skip like flat stones across the surface of a pond? How do we preach to victims of trauma without reviving the experience of the trauma? In her own poetic words, "What is a credible expression of the gospel for those who have experienced an absence of grace, especially when the imagination may be incapacitated, and language loosed from its moorings?" The goal is clear, to preach the gospel and the redeeming power of God's love, but getting there in a way that communicates empathy and builds trust is the challenge.

In response, some people say that psychology is important, and it is. Preachers are to be like God coming to us in Jesus Christ, they must enter into the pain, not just the pain of the other, but also the pain within themselves. Whatever words are said must speak first in a compelling way to the trauma and woundedness that the preacher may carry, before those words can be compelling for someone else. Self-awareness can make us aware of the self of others; it also prevents us from shifting the focus of preaching to ourselves.

Psychology on its own is not enough, however. Theology is the more central issue, as Travis makes clear, not least how we best shape what we do to be in service to the Holy Spirit. Whatever comfort for trauma we may offer as pastors, the Spirit is the true "Comforter" (John 14:26 KJV). Paul says that "faith comes through hearing," through proclaiming the good news in Jesus Christ. Jesus says that the Spirit gives us the words, "the Holy Spirit will teach you at that very hour what to say." (Luke 12:12). Even if our own words fail both us and our people, the Spirit can still find a way to deliver hope, though for us mainly to rely on that is like Jesus's temptation to leap from the pinnacle of the Temple and have God save him (Luke 4:9–12).

What is the gospel and how do we proclaim it? The word gospel literally means good news. Gospel may be understood as any saving act of God, anywhere in the Bible. Those saving acts can be seen most clearly in Jesus Christ: in God who has come to us in human form, in Jesus's ministry, death, resurrection, and in his Spirit guiding and strengthening us now and for the life to come.

What passes for good news in churches usually falls short. People are told what to do. Part of the good news is the instruction God gives to bring our behavior in line with God's will. But human action on its own is not the gospel. We cannot save ourselves or make ourselves righteous before God. Left to our own resources, we are likely to fail. To use the old words, sin and evil exist, and of our own free will, we keep being attracted to the wrong choices. That is the burden we bear. It is trouble. The fullness of the good news includes not just the instructions, but also the help God gives to enable us to do what is required. That is the burden God chose to bear in becoming human and dying for us. By our faith in Christ, the Spirit gives us his resurrection power of life over death. When the trouble is put alongside God's saving action, paired with it, that is the gospel. The movement of the sermon can be from trouble to grace in a gathering symphony of hope.

Travis gets this. She rightly asks, is there a danger that we push too quickly toward resurrection?

Gospel needs to be unpacked in relation to trauma and its specific contexts, we cannot simply paste a "Jesus died for us" bandage over the wounds. Indeed, trauma victims may not be able to hear about a loving God, or God may seem silent or absent to them. Travis conceives not of a direct linear progression from trouble to grace, but of a gap that allows for an intermingling of the two, a transitional space that acknowledges the ambiguity and confusion so many people feel in relation to faith. It is a gap between death and life, between Good Friday and Easter. She claims Holy Saturday as productive space and time in which the preacher can stand.

The pastoral issues around trauma are so complex and serious, it is important to follow Travis's lead and wrestle with how exactly to best proclaim the gospel to those burdened and broken by trauma. Partly arising out of her own powerful testimony, she gives practical suggestions about what might be helpful or hurtful to say to trauma victims. Maybe she is right, that intermingling the trouble and good news, that is, letting lament color the good news, is a realistic way to best address their needs. It is worth considering, because preachers must preach, and they have to use some rhetorical and theological strategies to communicate what is needed. This book will give valuable help to preachers in deciding what their strategy will be.

For myself, I agree that there is a wrong way to proclaim the gospel, in which it may no longer be good news. Preaching the resurrection as though everything is all better now is one of the wrong ways. Eschatology is essential. The good news of Easter is not "Good Friday doesn't matter and there will be no more death," nor is it that the Second Coming has already happened. The reality of death and sin still stand, the innocent one has been crucified, but God has determined that is not the end of the story. The end is launched in the resurrection, it is the beginning of the end.

Travis makes a point that belongs in every preaching class. The gospel ought never to be parachuted in, regardless of the setting in which it lands. Even in the Bible, Easter is not all celebration, it is a day of some confusion and dawning joyous belief. An intermingling is already present perhaps without importing more: the trouble on Easter morning can be Christ is risen— what we expected had the last say does not and our old ways of thinking need to change—and the good news on Easter is the same, Christ is risen—God opens a new future for us in Christ. In any case, gospel is always in relationship to the past, never isolated from it. God in love responds to human needs. This response starts in the specific details of the biblical text being preached. The text makes a claim about what God is doing, and the preacher lifts up that saving action and applies it to today.

Travis offers a vital challenge. In speaking to the unspeakable horrors of trauma, preachers must decide, whether to mute the gospel, in the trust and hope that that is a more pastoral route and more likely to be received, or not? A good case can be made for either strategy. In faith we might affirm that the Holy Spirit can make a miracle out of whatever offering is made.

I still want to hold out for a gospel best not muted. My own failures to dwell with the Word long enough, or deep enough, already mute it. The world, sin, evil, our brokenness, suffering, pain, and trauma mute it. In speaking truth to power—in this case often the power of the demonic—I want to hear in relation to my own pain a clear and unequivocal message that the power of death has been overcome in Christ. While the effect of trauma is still with us, its power has already been broken and it will not have the last word. Resurrection for some of us can be a slow process, perhaps in part for physiological reasons, our bodies are made that way and the body recovers in its own time. Yet already, even now, Christ is ministering to us in the Spirit and is making all things new, especially in the moment of proclamation. An unstoppable day is coming when unimaginable joy, healing, and restoration of relationships will be upon us. Maybe instead of a "not yet" gospel, we may present a "yet already" gospel, a new day dawned.

Paul Scott Wilson

Emeritus Professor of Homiletics
Emmanuel College of Victoria University in The University of Toronto

Acknowledgments

Writing about trauma is a difficult task. It was made easier by the cloud of witnesses that surrounded me and supported me. First, to my husband Paul Miller, who put up with my moaning and groaning about the difficulty of writing this book and acted as a constant cheerleader, as well as editor. To my children, Ben, Ella, and Olive, who gave me time and space to write and served as a continual inspiration to do my best work. To my colleagues at the Toronto School of Theology and Knox College, for their companionship and willingness to celebrate my successes with me. To the folks at Norval Presbyterian Church, for encouraging me to continue scholarship even as I minister among them. To Boghos Barbouri for reading portions of the manuscript and introducing me to the concept of Bibliodrama. To Lianne Biggar for her supremely careful copyediting. While I acknowledge that I couldn't have written this book without the help of others, all errors and omissions are my own.

Pentecost, 2020

Introduction

The Failure of Beautiful Words

In Advent 2017, I was writing a series of sample sermons for a denominational website. The Hebrew text for Advent 3, Year B, came from the prophet Isaiah (Isa 61:1–11). The prophet offers a spectacular vision of restoration, as those who mourn in Zion begin to heal and repair what has been devastated:

> They shall build up the ancient ruins, they shall raise up the former devastations; they shall repair the ruined cities, the devastations of many generations.[1]

It was one of those experiences of writing a sermon in which the words flowed until, suddenly, they stopped. Neither my tongue nor my brain could articulate a message of hope. I was unable to translate the good news of this text into a credible gospel for today. I simply could not find images of contemporary hope that were adequate to illustrate the magnitude of restoration promised by the prophet when compared to the magnitude of devastation experienced by so many in our world. I was stuck on images of Aleppo, Haiti, New Orleans . . . places where death, destruction, and ongoing trauma resist any easy hope. It seemed almost a sacrilege to dare to even whisper about restoration in spaces and places where restoration is not imminent or perhaps even possible. How can we imagine restoration in the face of traumatic realities? Restoration implies some kind of return to a former state, a return to the "before"; yet, with trauma, there is no going back to a pristine former state. Jennifer Baldwin, who writes about trauma-sensitive theology,

---

1. Isa 61:4 NRSV.

has suggested that "restoration is cultivating resiliency and repairing the wounds of the relational injury with or without restoring the relational connection between perpetrators and victim/survivors."[2] While I longed to say something in my sermon that would cultivate resiliency and the repairing of wounds, the words simply would not come.

Coincidently, serendipitously, I had earlier in the day printed an article written by Shelly Rambo, for an unrelated project. Rather than flail silently at my computer, I turned to the article, unexpectedly finding coherence and possibility for my sermon in Rambo's work on trauma. She writes about being in New Orleans twenty-nine months after Hurricane Katrina and discovering the "ongoingness" of trauma. She says, "Hurricane Katrina was not simply a singular event that took place in August 2005. It is an event that continues, that persists in the present. Trauma is what does not go away."[3] Rambo writes about theological silence in the face of traumatic events[4] and the danger that we "proclaim the good news before its time."[5] The life that emerges post-trauma is "uncertain, tentative and murky,"[6] and thus resists any easy attempt at restoration. Rambo's wisdom and experiences echoed in my own silence and brought to light the extent to which I was not "trauma-informed." I was frozen in my response to traumatized communities. The sermon on Isaiah was eventually written, but with a muted gospel. The only thing I could utter was a passive kind of ministry of presence:

> In our rush to make everything ok, to solve the problems,
> To seek resurrection from the dead,
> We might miss the opportunity to suffer with others.
> In this season, in-between death and life, life and death,
> A space opens up between pain and hope—
> A space in which we can stand with those who wait
> For something to change.
> In this unimaginable territory,

---

2. Baldwin, *Trauma-Sensitive Theology*, 117. Not all trauma is caused by relational injury. This book seeks to find a balance among those forms of trauma that are caused by relational injury, and those that have other causes, such as illness or natural disaster.

3. Rambo, "Spirit and Trauma," 8.

4. Rambo, "Spirit and Trauma," 8.

5. Rambo, "Spirit and Trauma," 9.

6. Rambo, "Spirit and Trauma," 19.

We are aware that there are sometimes no words
which will comfort.

Nothing we can do, nothing we can even imagine

That will bring new life where there is only the stench of death.

Instead, we are invited to wait, equipped only with the promise
of a faithful God

That life is indeed possible.

The good news here is that God wants more for us,

For all creation.[7]

While I was not content with the outcome of my sermon, it did create within me a desire to know more about how to preach in the face of trauma and the unspeakable events that destroy homes and lives.

This book wonders about the implications of traumatic experience for preaching. In particular, it looks at the theological implications of trauma, aiming to support preachers with a theological lens as they think through the effect of trauma on listeners and how this may impact the way that sermons are prepared and received. I was inspired to write this book by a young man who has experienced multiple traumas. He reminded me that beautiful words are not enough to atone for the effects of trauma. Safety cannot be restored with words but only at the level of the senses.[8] This is true whether the cause of trauma is relational injury or an unexplainable mystery. If safety cannot be restored by words alone, what does this mean for preaching that is so dependent on words? Annie Rogers claims that trauma has its own language—the language of the "unsayable."[9] What can we say in the face of unspeakable grief and trauma?

Trauma occupies the sanctuary. Perhaps more than ever before in history, because of the easy availability of global news, we are aware of the terrible things that occur. It is not necessary here to recount all the traumatic events that occupy our minds, but it is helpful to think about the various levels and categories of trauma that shape traumatic experience in the here and now. Types of trauma may be cultural, personal, collective, historical, institutional, or global. I want to be careful not to collapse or homogenize experience of trauma—not all traumas are equal; rather, their effects depend on the specifics of individual experience and

---

7. Travis, "Sermon, Advent 3."

8. Rambo, *Spirit and Trauma*, 163.

9. Rogers, *Unsayable*, title of book.

available resources for coping. Traumatic experience is not limited to war zones or plane crashes. Trauma happens in our homes, our neighborhoods, and our churches. It comes with the death of a loved one, it comes with relational abuse, it comes in the form of illnesses that spread through communities. None of us can escape its impact, regardless of the degree to which we are personally afflicted.

Preachers carry the stories of many: those known personally to us, as well as those that occupy the larger social space. When one begins to unpack the layers of trauma present in our culture and thus in our pews, it is astounding. As our communities become more multicultural, our awareness of postcolonial trauma is increased—war, terrorism, and oppression of all kinds. Today, there are millions of refugees roaming the planet, searching for a place to rest their heads. In my Canadian context, there is an awareness of generational and ongoing trauma among Indigenous populations that have been subordinated and disenfranchised by colonialism. Gun violence is a tremendous social evil that results in terrible fear and trauma for whole communities. Cultural experiences of racism and sexism result in traumatized populations, with trauma that often carries forward from generation to generation. In our pews, individuals suffer from the traumas produced by natural human experience—the death of loved ones, injury and illness, even childbirth. There are also traumas produced by others—including the traumas of domestic violence and sexual abuse.

Trauma impacts our life together as an ecclesial body. We preach not only to trauma survivors but also to those who have been impacted by the trauma experienced by others. Perhaps more difficult, we preach to those who have been perpetrators of trauma. Sometimes, we preach to communities that have been traumatized by terrible local events. Sometimes, as in the case of 9/11 or COVID-19, it is a whole nation that is traumatized and desperately seeking a word from the pulpit that is adequate to the situation. In the summer of 2020, the world was facing two pandemics: COVID-19 and the rise of anger about the treatment of black lives following the death of George Floyd in Minneapolis. COVID-19 separated us from each other, caused economic suffering, and created an atmosphere of fear rooted in the deaths that continually mounted. Churches faced various kinds of trauma as they were shut down and experienced economic and relational consequences. The death of George Floyd led to mass protests and a tidal wave of frustration and anger that swept across the nation and the world. Preachers everywhere struggled to find adequate responses to unimagined situations.

Preachers exist in communities that have diverse reactions and responses to traumatic events. What determines which people and communities will move forward and which communities are unable to imagine a way forward? Does preaching have a role to play in the manner in which communities respond to, and heal from, traumatic events?

Trauma and Theology

In her book *Trauma and Grace*, Serene Jones asks, "How can ministers craft sermons that speak to the plight of trauma survivors without retraumatizing them? How do we make theological sense of what happened on the cross in a way that speaks to the experience of traumatized victims without glorifying violence?"[10] This book takes up that challenge. As preachers, we are always trying to make meaning out of chaos. What theological resources can we draw on in order to lead toward healing? Rambo positions this work as a "two-world practice"—"it is the work of transfiguring the world—working between the *as is* and the *otherwise*."[11] This kind of transfiguration, or transformation, works at the levels of imagination and language, both of which are central to preaching.

At the most basic level, preaching must respond in some way to suffering—the suffering of those who are listening and the suffering experienced by others that invades our own lives through the news and social media. Preaching must respond to the deepest forms of human suffering and proclaim what God is doing, if anything, to alleviate suffering. It must name out loud such hope as is to be found.

Theology has always tried to answer questions of human suffering, and our theology must evolve alongside current understandings of trauma. "We must have the courage, confidence and clarity to re/form our theology and liturgy so that it continues to make use of the best knowledge of our time for the benefit, growth, and health of individuals, communities and society."[12] Thus, it is imperative that our theology and practice meet up with trauma theory. This is contextual theology—it begins in experience. When our theology and practice intersect with Christian theology, the task may involve rethinking some of the claims of Christian faith. Trauma shatters our most familiar frameworks of theology; it speaks of things we don't

10. Jones, *Trauma and Grace*, 85.

11. Arel and Rambo, *Post-Traumatic Public Theology*, 3.

12. Baldwin, *Trauma-Sensitive Theology*, 1.

5

necessarily want to hear or to know about the situation of others and the activity of God. In the words of Serene Jones, "How do people, whose hearts and minds have been wounded . . . come to feel and know the redeeming power of God's grace? At the heart of this question sits a vexing problem":

> When people are traumatized, a kind of cognitive/psychic overwhelming breakdown can occur. When this happens, it becomes difficult for victims to experience the healing power of God's grace because their internal capacities (where one knows and feels) have been broken. It is hard to know God when your knowing faculties have been disabled. It is hard to feel divine love when your capacity to feel anything at all has been shut down.[13]

While the church is a place in which many people are able to find connection and healing, it can sometimes be a place in which trauma is ignored or unalleviated. Baldwin writes, "The church, in its ignorance of traumatic processing is too often a place of misunderstanding and re-traumatization."[14] She goes on: "A theology that is ignorant of trauma process is more likely to harm than offer good news."[15]

Preaching and Trauma

Preaching is a healing discourse that proclaims gospel, or good news. Gospel is a complicated reality, especially in the face of trauma. Rambo writes that "the good news lies in the ability of Christian theology to witness between death and life, in its ability to forge a new discourse between the two."[16] So much of this is inarticulable—but what does preaching do with that which lies at the edges of our comprehension?[17] Trauma exceeds familiar logic—it shatters what we know about life and death and tests our articulation and comprehension of grace. As witnesses to both trauma and grace, we seek to name "presence and power in the places where life is least discernable."[18] How do we know ourselves, and know God, when our bodies and minds have experienced deep pain or violence? Trauma can do terrible things to

---

13. Jones, *Trauma and Grace*, xii.

14. Baldwin, *Trauma-Sensitive Theology*, 3.

15. Baldwin, *Trauma-Sensitive Theology*, 12.

16. Rambo, *Spirit and Trauma*, 8.

17. Rambo, *Spirit and Trauma*, 10.

18. Rambo, *Spirit and Trauma*, 13.

the human person, and preachers have a responsibility to understand and respond to the marks of trauma left on the souls of our listeners and our communities. Preaching has a role to play in creating safer communities.

Trauma has a tremendous impact on our relationship to grace and gospel. The primary task of Christian preaching is to express good news, but good news in the face of trauma is neither straightforward nor easily expressed. I was a student of Paul Scott Wilson, and like many other preachers in North America I have been influenced by his *The Four Pages of the Sermon*. It is a profoundly theological model of sermon preparation that focuses on God's action in the world and in the text. The trouble of the text and our world is viewed through the lens of God's gracious action. However, in the face of trauma, there is a pause, a disconnect, between trouble and grace. Even when we can perceive that God is acting, there is no easy movement from trouble to grace. Is this space between life and death, trouble and grace, perhaps productive?

The intent of this book is to equip preachers with an awareness of traumatic experience so that they may respond adequately to the trauma that is experienced by listeners, avoid retraumatizing, and participate in a healing discourse. Ultimately, there is grace given by a God who loves the world passionately, but how do we preach grace in the face of woundedness? Drawing on the work of theologians in conversation with trauma studies, such as Shelley Rambo and Serene Jones, and in conversation with homiletic and trauma literature, this book asks, What is a credible expression of the gospel for those who have experienced an absence of grace, especially when the imagination may be incapacitated, and language loosed from its moorings?

I am best situated to speak from the lens of practical theology and homiletics. As a preacher, I am always wondering how we begin to talk about the questions of suffering that occupy our minds and hearts. As a homiletician who works with postcolonial theories and the hope of decolonization, I am aware of the ways that colonial histories and legacies impact the lives of those to whom I preach, as well as the implications of oratory power. I have had intimate encounters with trauma in my own life, although I have not faced complex trauma—mine were discrete incidents that were always insulated by grace, such as a car accident and a life-threatening childbirth. There was one event, however, that stretched the limits of my capacity to cope with trauma.

On a bright and cold January day in 2006, I was in a staff meeting at the church where I worked. During that meeting, I received a phone message from my husband saying that my younger son had been taken to the hospital. I got in my car and drove—worried, but not desperately so. However, when I was ushered into the trauma room in the ER, the bottom dropped out of my world. Sam, then fifteen months old, was surrounded by doctors and respiratory therapists. There was a nurse in the corner desperately trying to record everything that the doctors were doing to save Sam's life. They resuscitated him four times. The pediatrician told us that there was a fifty-fifty chance of survival. A social worker appeared, and I recall being rude to her because, as a pastoral professional, I knew that the news was not good when they called in social work. My mind and my heart were reeling—how does this happen to a healthy, happy little boy? Surprisingly, amazingly, he opened his eyes and recognized us, but that was just the beginning of our journey. He recovered briefly from the initial onslaught but was to spend the next months in and out of hospital. Countless medical procedures, three liver transplants, two medical ambulance airlifts—this was the stuff of nightmares for me as a mother. My husband and I, and our community of family, friends, faith and medical staff, did everything we could to keep Sam alive. We pushed dozens of drugs into a feeding tube every day, we learned how to clean and protect his wounds, we prayed, we hoped. Nevertheless, the worst happened: Sam died of heart failure on his third birthday. The moments surrounding his death are still too painful to recount, but I remember one intensive-care nurse looking at me with tears in her eyes. She said, "I've been here. I've lost a child too." I responded, "but you are still here." It was a moment of profound gratitude and hope—it is possible to survive, and even thrive in the worst circumstances. This is a gift of grace.

Even a dozen years later, the smell of coffee in an elevator, the beeping of a hospital monitor, or the whir of an Air Ambulance can send me into a state of panic. I recall being in a worship service soon after Sam died. It was the season of Advent, and my grief was fresh and raw. I couldn't sing words of hope. As a preacher, I felt pressure to live out my faith publicly, but the experience of worship was too much for me. I walked out of that worship service—because I did not feel that there was space for my trauma.

Like many, I have needed space to contend with, and heal from, traumatic injury. Despite these events, I find myself always pushing toward resurrection—always looking for the flower inside the bulb or the butterfly inside the cocoon. This is a personal grace that I have endured suffering and yet continued to flourish. I wonder, though, how this grace has blinded me to the plight of others who cannot find resurrection, who cannot dare to hope because present reality is too painful? To push too quickly toward resurrection may be the least pastoral response imaginable.

I am a pastor and theologian, not a clinician. While I have tried to learn from the best writing of clinicians, this work is an attempt at a constructive theology for preaching—it is not a clinical discourse. "Trauma is bigger than expertise of any sort—it's in our midst, in our language, our wars, even the ways we try to love, repeating, repeating. No one is an expert on trauma."[19] There are of course those who know about trauma, those who have lived it, those who have studied it, those who have journeyed with others through the dark nights of the soul. This book draws on the insights of many in an attempt to untangle the strange grace of preaching to the traumatized.

Chapter 1 offers an introduction to trauma, its effects, and what is known about the potential to recover from trauma. This discussion of trauma is contextualized in the practice of preaching—what are the implications of trauma's effects for preaching itself, and how might the act of preaching play a role in the recovery of trauma, even lead toward posttraumatic growth?

Chapter 2 explores the theological implications of trauma for preaching and the ways we might need to reimagine our theologies in order to adequately address both trauma and hope. Considering the contours of a trauma-informed theology, I then explore the concept of gospel and what it may mean to preach a credible gospel in the face of trauma. This exploration leads toward an in-between space from which to consider life and death.

Chapter 3 asks what it might mean to preach toward healing and recovery from trauma while occupying an "in-between space." I explore the concept of "witness" as a central task for preaching, drawing on Shelly Rambo's concept of witnessing from the middle. Preachers are witnesses to trauma and witnesses to the gospel. How do we reconcile these two realities?

Chapter 4 considers the role of imagination in preaching, casting a vision for a future beyond trauma, including the tasks of crafting communal identity and embodying community through preaching. I employ the image of midwife to describe a manner in which the preacher can approach the task

---

19. Rogers, *Unsayable*, xiv.

of preparing and delivering sermons that aim to transform the pain and grief of trauma into something resembling new life.

Chapter 5 takes seriously the notion that biblical hermeneutics are essential for the task of preaching. This chapter introduces biblical scholarship at its intersection with trauma studies. I draw on the practice of Bibliodrama to demonstrate a concrete strategy for the preparation of sermons and consider lament as a hermeneutical framework that supports trauma-informed theology for preaching.

Trauma-informed preaching requires both courage and boldness: we "require courage to acknowledge the depth of trauma in our lives and society and a boldness to speak the truth when it is easier to remain silent or unaware."[20] It is likely a book that has more questions than answers, but it is intended to open a conversation that ultimately may lead to more sensitive and healing discourse in the pulpit and beyond. Grace is grace. It comes.[21]

20. Baldwin, *Trauma-Sensitive Theology*, 71.
21. Jones, *Trauma and Grace*, 74.

1

Defining Trauma and Its Effects

Fireworks are a popular and fun way to publicly celebrate the New Year, the birthday of a nation, even a holiday weekend. In my neighborhood, I am accustomed to hearing the familiar bang-bang of these beautiful lights. For some, these events are among the most exciting times of the year. For others, they can trigger traumatic responses. Refugees from war-torn countries and veterans may find fireworks to be a startling assault that takes them back to undesirable places in their memories, and they may hear shootings or bombs rather than the sounds of celebration. As one Syrian child who is a refugee to Canada noted, "The fireworks sound like bombs . . . It makes my head hurt and I feel scared."[1] Such is life after a traumatic event. One of the things trauma does is make people more sensitive to threat. Life becomes unsafe, as trauma creeps into the present and refuses to stay in the past.

This chapter attempts to define trauma, encompassing many of the ways that trauma finds its way into the body of the church. The term *trauma* means different things to different people, and my intent here is to define it as broadly as possible to include a full range of experiences and emotions. Some of what I write here is equally applicable to people who are mired in grief rather than what might be traditionally considered trauma. The descriptions of trauma offered below are necessarily brief, and where possible I have provided bibliographical references so that preachers can search deeper into the concepts presented.

There are obviously degrees of traumatic experience. Sometimes traumatic events are healed with relative ease; some are profound and have significant consequences for the long-term well-being of individuals and

---

1. Stewart and El Chaar, "Syrian Youth."

their communities. I am operating on the assumption that no one escapes traumatic violence—whether it lives in the soul, on the doorstep, or on one's neighbor's doorstep, we live in a world in which traumatic violence affects everyone. The following discussion considers definitions and effects of trauma, particularly in relation to the ways that they matter for the task of preaching. I consider the issues of which preachers need to be aware so that they may model open, compassionate, courageous, and curious leadership that can respond adequately to the presence of trauma.

Always in preaching, it is essential to think about who is listening—who are the co-interpreters of gospel? On any given Sunday morning, we preach among a multitude of others, including those who bear trauma in their bodies and souls. Some of this trauma is firsthand, driven by experiences of illness, abuse, or personal violence. Other trauma is brought on by witnessing the experiences of others. *Primary traumatization* affects those who witness a traumatic event or have a traumatic response to a direct personal experience. *Secondary traumatization* impacts those who are traumatized by the traumatic experience of someone else. This is also referred to as *indirect trauma* and might be experienced by therapists or caregivers who have listened to the stories and experiences of trauma described by their patients or those in their care. In some cases, we as preachers are well aware of the traumatic experiences of listeners. Our parishioners may have told us about their experiences of trauma, or we might have knowledge of the events that have shaped their lives. Sometimes, trauma is hidden in the deep recesses of the pews and we have no idea what is going on beneath the surface. Any time we climb into the pulpit, there will be listeners who are interpreting the gospel through the lens of their own traumatic experience.

Serene Jones tells the story of her young friend Leah, whom she is sponsoring for baptism. In the midst of a communion service, Leah is overcome with terror and flees the sanctuary. As Jones comes to realize the potential effects of the liturgical emphasis on body and blood, she begins to wonder about the traumatic experiences of others in the sanctuary. How could grace reach someone like Leah, who suffers from Post-Traumatic Stress Disorder (PTSD)? How can "liturgy, community, and faith together work best to encourage healing in broken places?"[2] Jones becomes aware of the presence of others affected by trauma: war veterans, a mother whose son died from drunk driving, a young girl who witnessed a drive-by shooting, a

---

2. Jones, *Trauma and Grace*, 8.

man from Rwanda, and possibly others whose trauma is hidden. Suddenly, the safe space of the sanctuary did not seem safe or orderly:

> What was most strange about this scene was that its chaos was unfolding . . . in the midst of worship itself. The belly-body of the sanctuary held all of it within its viscera; the liturgy moved in and through its midst, circulating through its aisles and around the many lives it held. At times, the words spoken, sung, or prayed struck violently against the fragile, traumatized people that gathered there, deepening the terror. I knew at once that such words and actions were not harbingers of grace but the spawn of the church's own brokenness and history of violence.[3]

The words, symbols, and practices of the Christian faith are loaded with traumatic imagery. Since trauma is present in our listeners and in our culture, preachers require training in trauma. They must learn about the ways that trauma shapes the experience of listeners and how those listeners will engage with God, with the church community, and with the gospel itself. Such training allows for "intentionality regarding interpretation and proclamation of scripture and theology"[4] and enables preachers to model leadership that is "open, compassionate, courageous and curious."[5] If preachers are to participate in healing,

> [they] must be equipped to recognize what can cause soul wounds; to understand how these deep wounds may affect relationships, participation in church, and worship; and how to preach in ways that minister not only to survivors of trauma but also to the many who struggle to find healing and meaning for disappointment, loss, and other painful experiences and memories.[6]

Jennifer Baldwin reminds us that clergy are the keepers of rituals that "mark and midwife us through life's significant milestones . . . providing meaning, witness and structure."[7] This task of midwifing is taken up later in this book. It is a task that involves courageous vulnerability on the part of the preacher as they provide meaning, witness, and structure in the face of trauma. I use the term *vulnerability* with intention. Preachers should at all times be aware of power issues, but never more so than when thinking

3. Jones, *Trauma and Grace*, 10.
4. Baldwin, *Trauma-Sensitive Theology*, 56.
5. Baldwin, *Trauma-Sensitive Theology*, 56.
6. Sancken, *Words That Heal*, §219–22.
7. Baldwin, *Trauma-Sensitive Theology*, 56–57.

through the trauma that is present in listeners. While the perceived authority of preachers has lessened in recent decades, preachers are still tasked with the privilege of standing up and witnessing before God's people and possess a high degree of relational power. Preaching is not, after all, egalitarian. Preaching in the midst of trauma requires preachers to approach the task with humility and vulnerability—fully aware of the power of words to build up or destroy. We are all vulnerable in the face of trauma—we cannot ever really know the experience of another, nor can we control or predict the effects of traumatic wounding, nor can we always participate in healing. This causes us to be vulnerable in the midst of forces that operate in our lives and world that transcend our human resources.

Trauma Theory

Trauma has always affected humanity, but the study of trauma is relatively new among the social and medical sciences. Judith Herman, in her classic text *Trauma and Recovery*, suggests that society as a whole has had episodes of amnesia regarding trauma—there have been periods in human history in which trauma has been ignored or dismissed.[8] The concept of trauma gained some traction because of the work of Sigmund Freud regarding the reliving of traumatic experience and therapists following patients exhibiting signs of shell shock after World War I. However, it wasn't until the 1970s that psychologists recognized that trauma outweighed the capacity for individuals to cope, particularly in response to events such as the Vietnam War and studies of sexual abuse. There emerged a field of research and analysis loosely called trauma studies. Trauma studies is a broad category that relates to medicine, psychology, sociology, literary criticism, and a variety of other fields. *Trauma* has become a keyword through which many professionals approach a variety of responses to violence and calamity.[9] The concept does not have a fixed meaning, but relates to "changing social constructions of experience, in the context of particular clinical, cultural, and political ideologies."[10]

A trauma surgeon focuses on trauma of the body, which is one of the reasons that we have come to understand trauma as a physical experience. However, the effects of trauma may be physical, psychological, relational,

8. Herman, *Trauma and Recovery*, 2.

9. Kirmayer et al., *Understanding Trauma*, 1.

10. Kirmayer et al, *Understanding Trauma*, 4.

or spiritual, and can affect individuals, families, communities, nations, and cultures. Serene Jones writes,

> The ancient Greek word for trauma, τραῦμα, means a "wound" or "an injury inflicted upon the body by an act of violence." To be traumatized is to be slashed or struck down by a hostile external force that threatens to destroy you. This visual image highlights the assaultlike character of a trauma; it involves an attack by an external agent upon a vulnerable human body in such a way that a wounding occurs.[11]

These woundings are not necessarily physical but generally involve some threat to the very being of a person. Only the individual can decide whether they have experienced a traumatic event. There is no agreed upon criteria for determining whether an event is traumatic: it is entirely dependent on how it is experienced and processed by the person. Thus, a traumatic reaction should be treated as valid and important, regardless of how the event that induced it appears to anyone else. While there is a possibility that the term *trauma* can be overused, it is impossible to determine, from the outside, whether someone has experienced a traumatic event. Trauma is defined by the way an individual responds to an experience, not the nature of the event itself. The degree of traumatization relates to the vulnerability of the person, as well as the degree to which they are supported, in addition to the severity of the event. Traumatic wounding occurs when a person's resources are outweighed by their vulnerability.[12] Trauma is different than stress—it is intense and overwhelming. It generally begins with physical threat or injury, but "violence often cuts so deeply into our minds that surface healings cover it over and, hidden away, allow it to expand."[13] Healing from these experiences is complex, and trauma can last for months or even years following the experiences that precipitated it.

Bessel van der Kolk argues that trauma, by its nature, is "unbearable and intolerable."[14] Traumatic events overwhelm ordinary human processes and make it difficult to cope: "Unlike commonplace misfortunes, traumatic events generally involve threats to life or bodily integrity, or a close personal encounter with violence and death. They confront human

---

11. Jones, *Trauma and Grace*, 12.

12. Baldwin, *Trauma-Sensitive Theology*, 27.

13. Jones, *Trauma and Grace*, ch. 1.

14. Van der Kolk, *Body Keeps Score*, 1.

beings with the extremities of helplessness and terror, and evoke the responses of catastrophe."[15]

Trauma can be said to occur when a reaction to an event negatively impacts the present, even long after the event has occurred. The event itself is not always accessible by the intellect or narratively—survivors may have trouble remembering or narrating the event as a whole; instead, they remember it in fragments and may struggle to name it out loud. Not only do traumatic events linger and haunt, but there are continually new experiences that lead to new trauma. These may be reminders of the initial event that trigger unformed memories, such as the sound of fireworks. To be overwhelmed by a traumatic event can be initially adaptive, resulting in altered states that help the victim bear the unbearable. However, at some point once the danger is past these responses become maladaptive "because these altered states keep the traumatic experience walled off from ordinary consciousness, they prevent the integration necessary for healing."[16]

Traumatic experiences are a kind of encounter with death. These encounters with death are not literal, but instead a manner of describing radical events that cause a disconnect from what an individual perceives to be safe and real in the world—they "shatter all that one knows about the world,"[17] and the event is understood as a "radical ending past which it is difficult, if not impossible, to conceive of life."[18]

A clinical presentation of trauma may be diagnosed as Post Traumatic Stress Disorder (PTSD), which was first recognized in 1980 by the American Psychiatric Association, although its definition and criteria for inclusion have expanded since that time.[19] The diagnostic criteria for PTSD include a history of exposure to a traumatic event and symptoms from each of three groups: intrusive recollections of the trauma event, avoidance of reminders of the event and emotional numbing, and hyperarousal. PTSD affects 3.5 percent of United States adults, and one in eleven will be diagnosed in a lifetime.[20] PTSD has "become more than a diagnostic label for individual suffering, it has become a way of naming the conditions of life more broadly."[21]

---

15. Herman, *Trauma and Recovery*, 33.

16. Herman, *Trauma and Recovery*, 45.

17. Rambo, *Spirit and Trauma*, 4.

18. Rambo, *Spirit and Trauma*, 4.

19. American Psychiatric Association, *DSM-V*, 271–80.

20. American Psychiatric Association, "What Is Posttraumatic Stress Disorder?"

21. Arel and Rambo, *Post-Traumatic Public Theology*, 9.

It results in actual physical, anatomical changes, especially in the case of developmental trauma. In PTSD patients, "the stress hormone system fails at this balancing act. Fight/flight/freeze signals continue after the danger is over, and . . . do not return to normal."[22] A person with PTSD may be "tormented by memory and bounded by helplessness and fear."[23]

There are different kinds of trauma, with a variety of different responses and related experiences. While we might be most likely to think about car accidents, attacks, war, abuse, and illness as categories of traumatic events, there are many other ways that individuals and communities are affected by trauma. Traumatic wounding occurs "visibly, dramatically, acutely, subtly, perniciously, chronically, relationally, systematically, and across all demographic categories."[24] While preachers, like others, may tend to recognize trauma in its most familiar forms and demographics, such as the experience of a significant accident or witnessing a murder, we might miss the less traditional ways in which trauma manifests itself. Baldwin notes that not all people reach the level of clinical presentation of trauma—many experience it at a sub-clinical level in which the individual is able to hold things together "well-enough."[25] These people also require care and support, and it may be that many of the individuals sitting in our pews have experienced such levels of trauma of which we are not aware. Trauma often occurs following a single, discrete event but can also occur following repeated, low-intensity negative situations, such as in the case of domestic abuse, a long illness, or a hostile workplace. Of course, some individuals and communities face repeated, long-term threats such as the threat of gun violence or the consistent threat of food insecurity.[26] These kinds of traumas that persist over time can be labeled *complex trauma*.

Maltreatment and trauma in the early years of a child's life can reshape their brain and interfere with normal development—a phenomenon called *developmental trauma*.[27] It can be brought on by "having a parent with mental illness or substance abuse, losing a parent due to divorce, death, abandonment or incarceration, witnessing domestic violence, not feeling loved or that the family is close, or not having enough food or clean

---

22. Van der Kolk, *Body Keeps Score*, 30.

23. Herman, *Trauma and Recovery*, 49.

24. Baldwin, *Trauma-Sensitive Theology*, 38.

25. Baldwin, *Trauma-Sensitive Theology*, 31.

26. Jones, *Trauma and Grace*, ch. 1.

27. Van der Kolk, *Body Keeps Score*, ch. 10.

clothing, as well as direct verbal, physical or sexual abuse."[28] Developmental trauma can lead to a sense of worthlessness, self-loathing, and lack of trust that persists through the lifespan.[29]

Participatory trauma occurs when individuals participate in situations that lead to the wounding or disruption of other individuals or communities. This is also called *moral injury* and may be most common in members of the military and first responders. "Moral injury is a loss injury; a disruption in our trust that occurs within our moral values and beliefs. Any events, action or inaction transgressing our moral/ethical beliefs, expectations and standards can set the stage for moral injury."[30] Romeo Dallaire, the United Nations's former peacekeeping commander in Rwanda, has been open about his struggles with PTSD following the peacekeeping mission. "Dallaire, a soldier with a mission to protect and orders not to intervene, had to stand by as up to a million people were killed in 100 days. Already, in the immediate aftermath, Dallaire couldn't sleep. His right arm was mysteriously fluctuating between sharp pain and paralysis. A voice in the back of his head was incessantly screaming, 'Why is the rest of the world carrying on like nothing has happened?'"[31]

Trauma affects whole societies as well as individuals. It is important to talk about the systematic and collective dimensions of trauma—social, institutional, and political. Psychological models of trauma have sometimes underestimated the degree to which trauma can arise amid social structures, placing too much emphasis on the individual.[32] Systematic oppressions such as poverty and racism can cause traumatic responses. In the case of indigenous peoples, for example, "transgenerational transmission at both individual and collective levels may link current social and mental health problems to the effects of colonization and policies of forced assimilation, in what has been called historical trauma."[33] Here, one might think about the historical and ongoing effects of apartheid in South Africa or slavery in the United States.

Judith Herman references the women's liberation movement that swept through Western society in the 1970s. Women began to speak out about

28. "What is Developmental Trauma."

29. Van der Kolk, *Body Keeps Score*, 158.

30. Kamkar, "Moral Injury."

31. Bethune, "Romeo Dallaire's Ongoing Battle."

32. Hess, *Sites of Violence*, 4.

33. Kirmayer et al., *Understanding Trauma*, 10.

their experiences of sexual abuse and trauma. "Through them, we realized the power of speaking the unspeakable and witnessed firsthand the creative energy that is released when the barriers of denial and repression are lifted."[34] These unspeakable things were released into the ether, encouraging others to come forward with their stories. They reflect the deeper and darker events that shape the lives not only of individuals but also of whole cultures. The "Me Too" movement is a contemporary example that demonstrates the degree to which sexual trauma can pervade an entire society.

Trauma can be passed down from generation to generation. This kind of intergenerational trauma is perhaps most fully described in the literature related to the Holocaust. Intergenerational transmission of trauma can be passed from parent to child to grandchild. This can occur in a number of ways—for example, a child might be frightened by a parent's story, a child may be affected by the symptoms of a parent, or a parent's trauma might impact the quality of caregiving they provide.[35]

We live in a time in which our listeners are likely to be diverse. Those with whom we interpret the gospel in preaching come from all over the world, and will, of course, have diverse experiences of trauma. One of the outcomes of such globalization is postcolonial trauma—those traumatic events that occurred within the context of colonialism and imperialism. Postcolonialism is a perspective that privileges the ways that colonialism and imperialism shape the experience of individuals and cultures that have been subject to the rule or tyranny of other groups. It relates to class and race. Trauma can be caused by colonialism and the resultant dislocation, diaspora, and experiences of violence as individuals and families are negatively impacted by colonial forces. For example, forced migration creates refugee populations that not only suffer from the experiences they left behind but also must navigate new systems that push the limits of their capacity to cope. In my Canadian context, the relationship between white, settler Canadians and indigenous peoples has been fraught, resulting in communities who suffer not only the memory of traumatization but also ongoing struggles to merely survive in under-resourced communities. In the nineteenth and twentieth centuries, the Canadian government operated dozens of schools for indigenous children. Children were removed from their families, stripped of their cultural norms, such as language, and often faced abuse. Residential School Syndrome is a diagnosis applied to some

34. Herman, *Trauma and Recovery*, 2.
35. Kirmayer et al., *Understanding Trauma*, 10.

Indian residential school students that includes "recurrent intrusive memories, nightmares, occasional flashbacks, and quite striking avoidance of anything that might be reminiscent of the Indian residential school experience . . . strikingly, there is a persistent tendency to abuse alcohol or sedative medication drugs, often starting at a very young age."[36]

In addition to the traumatic events themselves, "public events of violence often expose the fragility of existing infrastructures of support."[37] Hurricane Katrina is a dramatic example of this phenomenon. "Katrina the 'natural disaster' revealed to the nation the 'manmade disaster' that existed in plain sight of Mardi Gras," namely the enduring structures of racism and poverty in the United States.[38] It disproportionally affected the elderly and African Americans[39] because of increased exposure and lack of access to resources. A *New York Times* article in 2006 stated, "New Orleans is experiencing what appears to be a near epidemic of depression and post-traumatic stress disorders, one that mental health experts say is of an intensity rarely seen in this country. It is contributing to a suicide rate that state and local officials describe as close to triple what it was before Hurricane Katrina struck."[40] One woman comments on her distress: "I thought I could weather the storm, and I did—it's the aftermath that's killing me . . . When I'm driving through the city, I have to pull to the side of the street and sob. I can't drive around this city without crying."[41]

Globalization has increased not only the occurrence of conflict and catastrophe but also our awareness of global events and the suffering of others. Trauma can be prompted "by a crisis event that is experienced either in person or via prolonged media coverage, on a mass scale."[42] Social media has heightened our proximity to the terror of others. Parents all over the world were adversely affected by the shootings and deaths of children at the Sandy Hook Elementary School in 2012 in Connecticut. Such events can lead to a sense of being less powerful but more present. In other words, we encounter the trauma of others and it affects the way we live our own lives, and yet we are removed enough from the situation that there is little

36. Brasfield, "Residential School Syndrome."

37. Arel and Rambo, *Post-Traumatic Public Theology*, 10.

38. Allen, "Katrina," 466.

39. Allen, "Katrina," 466.

40. Saulny, "Legacy of the Storm."

41. Saulny, "Legacy of the Storm."

42. Baldwin, *Trauma-Sensitive Theology*, 34.

we can do to support those experiencing trauma. In September 2015, major news outlets carried the story of Alan Kurdi, a little boy from Syria who drowned in the Mediterranean Sea while his family was fleeing to safety. This image appeared over and over again in social media, and my husband and I had a very difficult time processing and responding to this image, perhaps because our son had died at a similar age. That event connected with our own trauma and triggered uncomfortable memories. However, such a personal connection is not required in order to be traumatized by such an image. We live in an age where dead children may be broadcast into our homes and onto our phones in an instant, and we cannot escape the traumatic underpinnings of these experiences.

The Effects of Trauma

Baldwin describes traumatic events as tipping points:

> [They] knock us off balance and demand a rethinking and reformation of our most deeply held assumptions about our life and the world. The ripple effect of traumatic wounding begins at the time of traumatic incidence in our physiology, gets held somatically in the cells and tissues of our body, becomes stuck in our brain's mechanism for processing in full, raises questions about relationships that were insufficient in protection, and prompts wondering about how the world works and God's role in it. The intensity of this ripple effect can range from that of a rough wave to a catastrophic tsunami.[43]

Trauma fundamentally reorganizes the perception of the mind and brain. Trauma tends to be carried not only in the mind but also in the body—"inside the bones."[44] "It changes not only how we think and what we think about, but also our very capacity to think."[45] Responses to traumatic events vary widely from individual to individual, but scholars and clinicians have traced a variety of physical, behavioral, and psychological symptoms. Not every traumatized person will display each symptom; symptoms will differ depending on a number of factors. Trauma can disrupt the integration of memories, the ability to create coherent personal narratives, the establishment of healthy relationships, and the ability to construct life-giving

43. Baldwin, *Trauma-Sensitive Theology*, 44.

44. Organ, "Speaking the Grief."

45. Van der Kolk, *Body Keeps Score*, 21.

visions for the future. The following section highlights some of the areas in which traumatized persons experience difficulty. These categories are loose and overlapping, and not exhaustive, but there are common patterns of response.

Memory

Memory does not work like a video camera. We remember events in a manner that depends on our attention, perception, and cognitive functioning. Those experiencing traumatic events "record" memories in different ways. Trauma survivors may not remember the event as a cohesive narrative but encounter it in fragments—possibly with no beginning and no end. In this sense, the memory is incomplete or unfinished and often intrudes into the present: "Trauma survivors live not with memories of the past, but with an event that could not and did not proceed through to its completion, has no ending, attained no closure, and therefore, as far as its survivors are concerned, continues into the present and is current in every respect."[46]

Intrusive memories are a hallmark of trauma for many survivors—flashbacks that may either relive the memory or immerse the survivor in fragments of images, smells, sensations that relate to the memory. For some, this reliving of memories helps them integrate the memory into their life story. For others, the memory doesn't fade or become integrated: it remains an intrusive and painful reliving that interferes with life in the present. "The central problem of trauma is a temporal one. The past does not stay, so to speak, in the past. Instead, it invades the present, returning in such a way that the present becomes not only an enactment of the past but an enactment about what was not fully known or grasped."[47]

Herman tells of a soldier who denied having traumatic experiences in the war. With treatment, he was able to remember the sinking of his ship in icy waters, but his memory was devoid of emotion and meaning. The patient "did not allow himself to think" about the terror and pain of the event.[48] This kind of suppression of memory is common in victims of trauma.[49] Others experience a sense of dissociation, as if the event happened to someone else (depersonalization) or was unreal/didn't really happen

46. Felman and Laub. *Testimony*, 69.
47. Rambo, *Spirit and Trauma*, 19.
48. Herman, *Trauma and Recovery*, 45.
49. Herman, *Trauma and Recovery*, 46.

(derealization). This is a defense mechanism that can be helpful to protect the individual from the full impact of the traumatic event, but eventually this failure to integrate the experience into one's psychological framework can cause tremendous discomfort.

It is common for victims of trauma to find themselves oscillating between extreme states. Survivors may experience amnesia coupled with intense floods of memory, or feeling overwhelming emotion alternating with periods of no feeling at all. Such instability exacerbates the sense of unpredictability and helplessness experienced by the traumatized person.[50] Those who have experienced trauma may turn to substance abuse or other forms of numbing in order to cope with the unease and pain associated with their trauma: "It takes tremendous energy to keep functioning while carrying the memory of terror, and the shame of utter weakness and vulnerability."[51] The traumatized person can experience a compulsion to repeat the violence by playing the memory over and over again, not necessarily as a complete image or story, but in fragments.

These problems related to memory have an impact on how and what we preach. We might be tempted to perceive time in a linear fashion as though the past stays in the past and the present and future are untethered to past events. However, survivors may continue to experience the past seeping into the present. Preaching can so often be about moving on—in Paul's words from Philippians, "forgetting what is past,"[52] or Isaiah's words, "Do not remember the former things."[53] We might believe that we are encouraging our listeners to move forward in a positive direction, but this may not be possible for some survivors of trauma. They may wonder why they are stuck—unable to move beyond the fragmented memories of that trauma.

Another possibility is that preaching can trigger memories. While we want our sermons to be vivid and lively, we might unintentionally trigger memories through our retelling of traumatic events in our culture. As will be discussed later on, it is important for preachers to witness to trauma as it occurs in our pews and in the wider society. It is also important for preachers to be aware of the kind of reactions they might unwittingly produce in their hearers. This might be especially true when preaching texts that witness to traumatic events in the biblical sphere. In my introductory

50. Herman, *Trauma and Recovery*, 47.

51. Van der Kolk, *Body Keeps Score*, 2.

52. Phil 3:13 NRSV.

53. Isa 43:18 NRSV.

preaching class, students are always assigned one text that they work with through the whole semester. One year, the text was Matthew 2—Herod's killing of the young children in Bethlehem. When I assigned the text, I did not think about the traumatic implications of this text for parents who have lost children—even though I am such a parent. Such a text can trigger memories and emotions that are extremely painful for some listeners.

Language

Trauma changes one's relationship to language. According to Annie Rogers, trauma "enters our speech as if by stealth, through the back door, in the night."[54] Trauma interferes with our typical narrative processes and can incapacitate language, leaving survivors without words to describe what they have experienced. This may be because of an error in cognitive processing; it may also be because there simply are not words to describe what has happened in situations that exceed our ability to comprehend and enunciate. Traumatic experiences often defy our ordinary, everyday terms and explanations. Primo Levi writes in relation to the Holocaust, in everyday life

> we say "hunger," we say "tiredness," "fear," "pain," we say "winter"
> ... [These] are free words, created and used by free men who lived
> in comfort and suffering in their homes. If the Lagers had lasted
> longer a new, harsh language would have been born; and only this
> language could express what it means to toil the whole day in the
> wind, with the temperature below freezing, wearing only a shirt,
> underpants, cloth jacket and trousers, and in one's body nothing
> but weakness, hunger and knowledge of the end drawing nearer.[55]

Annie Rogers offers another example from her work with children who had experienced profound suffering: "Some of the children I met eventually spoke directly about a story of suffering, as [Alesha] did, and yet their stories remained beyond their words. Most of the children I saw did not speak plainly to me, and many had to find another avenue, another expression, to discover their way into speech."[56] Rogers, in discussing what she saw in her young patients, discovered that what is so terrible about trauma might not be the actual abuse but "the way terror marks the body and then becomes

---

54. Rogers, *Unsayable*, xiv.
55. Levi, *Survival in Auschwitz*, 123.
56. Rogers, *Unsayable*, §51.

invisible and inarticulate."[57] According to Bessel Van der Kolk, trauma "drives us to the edge of comprehension, cutting us off from language based on common experience or an imaginable past."[58]

Preaching is especially vulnerable to the effects of trauma when it comes to trouble processing language. After all, our sermons are composed of words that are intended to convey specific meanings and intentions. If we are to preach about traumatic experiences or traumatic texts, it is very important to consider the ways that we use language—"the language we use to describe our experiences can exaggerate, minimize or accurately reflect the significance and impact of what occurs."[59] Preaching relies on the language of the everyday, and cannot possibly express what has been experienced by some listeners and some communities. At the same time, preaching can narrate such events in such a way that they become more comprehensible and articulable.

Hope, Imagination, and Meaning-Making

As Serene Jones writes, trauma can "override your powers of both action and imagination."[60] Trauma is disorienting and overwhelming. It outstrips our capacity to cope, our sense of agency, and overwhelms our meaning-making capacity. It can therefore override the power of imagination to extract us from the perils of the particular moment. Imagination consists of the "thought stories" that help us to interpret ourselves and our world.[61] Traumatic events interfere with our imagination and our ability to tell life-giving stories. We might become stuck in the stories of the past and unable to imagine a future. We might be incapable of acting in effective and forward-looking ways. Judith Herman reports a study about kidnapped schoolchildren by Terr: "Years after the event, the children retained a foreshortened sense of the future; when asked what they wanted to be when they grew up, many replied that they never fantasized or made plans for the future because they expected to die young."[62] As Rambo writes, "The linear framework of past, present and future is a way

57. Rogers, *Unsayable*, §44.

58. Van der Kolk, *Body Keeps Score*, 43.

59. Baldwin, *Trauma-Sensitive Theology*, 23.

60. Jones, *Trauma and Grace*, 15.

61. Jones, *Trauma and Grace*, 20.

62. Herman, *Trauma and Recovery*, 46–47.

of orienting oneself in time. When this orientation is lost, what grounds persons and communities in the world?"[63] It is this sense of living the past in the present that is one of the most difficult aspects of coping with trauma. Trauma returns—in more extreme cases in flashbacks, but it may also persist in a sadness that will not go away.

The past does not stay in the past, but sneaks into the present, potentially dismantling any hope for a future that is beyond the past. Trauma impairs the ability to imagine the future—which has tremendous implications for preaching that seeks to guide listeners toward new life. Trauma interferes with "how one conceives of imagination, recognizing that at any moment haunting, shadowy scenes of violence can disrupt it, twist it, and shut it down."[64] It may be that listeners are unable to imagine a future at all, and our sermons which are so carefully crafted to help listeners imagine a future that is different from the present may fall on unhearing ears. For example, many preachers end sermons with an application—a means for listeners to go into the world and apply the learnings from Scripture and theology. Trauma survivors may struggle to make positive changes based on our sermonic urgings.

The theological frameworks used to help those who have experienced trauma make sense of the way the world works may be shut down, impaired, or turned upside down. At the same time, faith can contribute to the process of searching for meaning, which leads to positive outcomes for trauma survivors. It is good news for preachers that faith can lead to positive outcomes, but listeners may have trouble connecting to our theological frameworks. For example, it might be difficult for a person suffering from the aftermath of a trauma to even imagine the abstract concept of hope. This will vary based on an individual's capacity to access a sense of resiliency in the moment.

Interpersonal

Traumatic experiences affect relationships to self and others, calling into question basic human relationships and destroying attachment to community, friends, and family, as well as society at large. "They shatter the construction of the self that is formed and sustained in relation to others. They undermine the belief systems that give meaning to human experience.

63. Arel and Rambo, *Post-Traumatic Public Theology*, 7.

64. Jones, *Trauma and Grace*, 11.

They violate the victim's faith in a natural or divine order and cast the victim into a state of existential crisis."[65] The world thus becomes unsafe, and relationships become unreliable. It becomes difficult, if not impossible, to engage in intimate relationships—"after you have experienced something so unspeakable, how do you learn to trust yourself or anyone else again? Or, conversely, how can you surrender to an intimate relationship after you have been brutally violated?"[66] One can imagine how potentially alienating and isolating this experience can be. Many traumas are not caused by human beings—they occur as a result of forces that still seem mysterious, despite our understanding of science and medicine. When trauma occurs with intention by loved one or stranger, it has an even greater impact on one's capacity to trust others and locate safe spaces in the world. Even relationships unconnected to the trauma are affected in the aftermath of trauma:

> Traumatized people feel utterly abandoned, utterly alone, cast out of the human and divine systems of care and protection that sustain life. Thereafter, a sense of alienation, of disconnection, pervades every relationship, from the most intimate familial bonds to the most abstract affiliations of community and religion. When trust is lost, traumatized people feel that they belong more to the dead than to the living.[67]

Individuals may view the world as an enemy, a hostile environment that has failed to keep them safe.[68] They may find it hard to be loved, which can result in the construction of a kind of interpersonal armor that protects the individual from seeing, and being seen by others.

Trauma has a profound impact on our capacity to trust God, others, and ourselves. This lack of trust may be especially evident toward those who did not experience the traumatic event.[69] Survivors of trauma may feel isolated and alienated, wondering how anyone can possibly understand what they have been through. How can they know? Jennifer Baldwin warns about caregivers and others privileging their own experience over that of the one who suffers. She defines *social privilege* as being able to navigate life safely without fear.[70] This privilege belongs to those who have not suffered

---

65. Herman, *Trauma and Recovery*, 51.

66. Van der Kolk, *Body Keeps Score*, 13.

67. Herman, *Trauma and Recovery*, 52.

68. Arel and Rambo, *Post-Traumatic Public Theology*, 10.

69. Van der Kolk, *The Body Keeps Score*, 18.

70. Baldwin, *Trauma-Sensitive Theology*, 77.

from trauma. When preachers fail to recognize that it is indeed a privilege not to have to live one's life in the space of traumatic wounding, they can cause additional harm. Preachers, in general, do not have to devote the same energy to self-protection and survival as do trauma survivors. Like other forms of social privilege, the privilege of non-traumatization can create a divide in human community, facilitating "a blindness to the reality of traumatic wounding that buffers those who have privilege from those who are wounded."[71] In extreme cases, a preacher might simply assume that these kinds of things "do not happen in my congregation."

Self and Identity

Traumatic events not only lead to alienation from others, but also can lead to alienation from oneself and one's identity. Trauma shatters the self, as the self has become a site of harm.[72] Self-blame is a common response to trauma, perhaps as a means to gain some control over what seems to be an uncontrollable situation. There is a loss of predictability and safety, and thus a sense of powerlessness regarding how one will function in a world that is no longer safe or predictable. One response can be shame, which is "a response to helplessness, the violation of bodily integrity, and the indignity suffered in the eyes of another person. Doubt reflects the inability to maintain one's own separate point of view while remaining in connection with others. In the aftermath of traumatic events, survivors doubt both others and themselves. Things are no longer what they seem."[73] Traumatized people may also be haunted by shame about their initial response to the traumatic event—they may regret their actions or inactions, or despise themselves for the myriad of emotions they felt (or didn't feel) at the time.[74]

How do we preach to those whose identities have been displaced, those who feel a sense of powerlessness and lack of agency? Agency relates to how we use the power we possess. Listeners may not feel that they have any power at all to change their circumstances. An important aspect of preaching is promoting change—we expect our sermons to accomplish something in the lives of our hearers. Trauma survivors may feel that they

---

71. Baldwin, *Trauma-Sensitive Theology*, 78.

72. Hess, *Sites of Violence*, 3–4.

73. Herman, *Trauma and Recovery*, 53.

74. Van der Kolk, *Body Keeps Score*, 13.

are beyond redemption,[75] as one can never go back to before the traumatic event. The event may not be the end of the world, but "it is the end of *a* world."[76] As will be discussed in subsequent chapters, preaching may have a role in creating a new world in which the person who has experienced traumatic wounding may find a place and space to act in positive ways toward healing and recovery.

Post-Traumatic Growth

The fictional superhero Batman is a prime example of trauma leading to growth. As a child, Bruce Wayne's parents are brutally murdered before his eyes. This leads him to develop a peculiar sense of justice, and he vows to fight against criminals. This, of course, results in his many adventures as Batman, the savior of Gotham: "I swear by the spirits of my parents to avenge their deaths by spending the rest of my life warring on all criminals."[77] As the years pass, Bruce Wayne prepares himself for his career. He trains his body to physical perfection until he is able to perform amazing athletic feats. The original comic reads:

> Dad's estate left me wealthy. I am ready but first I must have a disguise.
>
> Criminals are a superstitious cowardly lot, so my disguise must be able to strike terror into their hearts. I must be a creature of the night, black, terrible, a . . . a . . .
>
> As if in answer, a huge bat flies in the open window!
>
> A bat! That's it! It's an omen . . . I shall become a bat!
>
> And thus is born this weird figure of the dark . . . This avenger of evil: The Batman.[78]

There is no doubt that trauma changes people—even the very structures of their brains. However, there is evidence that the change is not always negative. Research shows that about half of people who experience trauma find themselves changed for the better.[79] In this sense, trauma can be an

---

75. Van der Kolk, *Body Keeps Score*, 2.

76. Baldwin, *Trauma-Sensitive Theology*, 30.

77. University of Colorado Boulder, "Batman Original Story."

78. University of Colorado Boulder, "Batman Original Story."

79. Rendon, *Upside*, §117.

opportunity for change, even a chance to develop a hope for the future that was not present before the traumatic experience. Traumatic events can be transformative, not simply hardships to overcome. The trauma can create a kind of dividing line in the life of an individual—they become different after the event. That change can be very negative, as in the case of PTSD, yet not all changes are negative. "Trauma survivors are often pushed by a brush with their own mortality, by the depth of their hardship or even the suffering of others, to find more meaningful and fulfilling ways of understanding who they are and how they want to live. They struggle, but they also change for the better."[80] In this case, suffering becomes part of a much larger experience and can prove to be "a kind of catalyst that pushed people to find new meaning in their lives."[81]

Tedeschi and Calhoun discovered that some people who had experienced seismic events in their lives reported positive change in the following areas: increased inner strength, an openness to new possibilities in life, closer and often deeper relationships with friends and family, and an enhanced appreciation for life and a stronger sense of spirituality.[82] For these individuals, trauma becomes an opportunity to find a new and better narrative for their lives. It is this ability to revise one's identity and re-tell the stories of their lives that creates a space for post-traumatic growth. It seems that such growth tends to be most common among those who have experienced a modest trauma—if the trauma is too great, an individual may not have enough left to rebuild. At the same time, a mildly traumatic event may not shake the individual to the core, and therefore does not present the opportunity for introspection and profound change.[83] Tedeschi writes,

> If a person is like a building built to a high standard to withstand an earthquake, if the quake comes and the building is still standing, you are okay. But if the building suffers damage, it has to be rebuilt and the rebuilding is the growth. Not everyone grows from traumatic experiences. But those who do are able to see that the horror and misery of trauma also create the opening for change . . . The challenge is to see the opportunity presented by this seismic event. In the aftermath of the earthquake, why not build

---

80. Rendon, *Upside,* §108.

81. Quoted in Rendon, *Upside,* §323

82. Quoted in Rendon, *Upside,* §323–29.

83. Quoted in Rendon, *Upside,* §863.

something better? Don't just live beneath the rubble, don't just build the same crappy building that you had before.[84]

Some individuals are able to climb out of the rubble and build a new and stronger building than they had before the traumatic event. Preaching can support such individuals in rebuilding and reconstructing the personal narratives of their lives.

Conclusion

The bottom line, according to Judith Herman, is that "no one can face trauma alone."[85] The preaching event gives us time and space to be with those who suffer and possibly to offer sparks of hope that can invade the darkness of traumatic wounding. There is much that preachers can do to be wise and generous companions on the road, and there are also many pitfalls to avoid along the way. The next chapter analyzes various theological concepts in relation to trauma, seeking a credible means for preaching the gospel to those who carry traumatic wounds on their bodies and souls.

84. Quoted in Rendon, *Upside*, §355.
85. Herman, *Trauma and Recovery*, 153.

2

Wounded Gospel: Preaching, Trauma, and Theology

I had the experience of talking with a friend who had lived through many traumatic events, including multiple forms of abuse and the dislocating pain of being a refugee. While I tried to listen carefully and compassionately, I couldn't seem to stop the urge to step in and fix the problem. Even in the face of such an horrific history, my whole being wanted to ask, "What about the gospel? What about resurrection?" I wanted to jump from crucifixion to resurrection. It was intolerable for me to watch the suffering happen. In my white, Western, privileged mind, I wanted the suffering to go away, to be swept away, wiped clean, by resurrection. Perhaps this is a preacher's urge, and yet "in our daily living, it is Pollyanna-ish to think trauma can always be conquered, but there's that continuing resistance to letting it be the final word. For so many, the lived experience of it in resurrection is never going to be the case."[1] If there is resurrection, trauma does not disappear. We still carry the wounds and scars on our bodies and souls.

A central task of trauma-informed preaching is to call into question our familiar theological frameworks—testing and adjusting them in order to account for the trauma that remains despite, or perhaps alongside, the good news of Jesus Christ. While the redemptive claims that lie at the heart of the gospel are profoundly good news, it may be that we need to reexamine them in order to find a more nuanced hope for trauma survivors. Christ leads to healing, but it is the wounded Christ that leads to healing. The hope that lies in the gospel is an "unreasonable" hope; it lies beyond the realm of what is normally possible.[2] This is good news for trauma survivors, in that

1. Jones in Rambo, "Theologians Engaging Trauma," 227.
2. Sancken, *Words That Heal*, §470–71.

healing and transformation are indeed possible. However, the gospel may be experienced "as provisional or partial, a foretaste of greater and deeper healing and joy found in God's horizon."[3]

According to pastoral theologian Deborah Hunsinger, in the resurrection "the powers of sin and death that have such a hold on us—*and that are at the root of all trauma*—are finally nullified."[4] I am reluctant to claim such healing in an uncritical manner, considering the trauma that remains in the souls and bodies of those who have suffered. If the powers of sin and death are truly nullified, we would not live in a world where so many carry the burden of pain and in which traumatic events continue to occur. I heartily affirm that transformation is possible, but it is not enough to naively claim total redemption and restoration because of a risen Christ. Shelly Rambo pays attention to the wounds that remain on Jesus when he appears to his disciples in the Upper Room.[5] The risen Christ continues to bear the marks of violence and trauma—they have not disappeared even in his return to life. Thus, the resurrection mollifies trauma but does not nullify it. In its redemptive promises, theology must account for those who suffer—their suffering "testifies to the unrealized promise."[6]

Trauma turns life inside out and upside down. Theology helps us to make sense of life, but in the face of trauma Christian theologies require careful consideration. Trauma itself becomes a lens for critiquing and analyzing existing theological frameworks. Trauma calls into question our assumptions about the nature of God, our theological anthropology, and our very understanding of time, future, and hope.

The central narrative of Christian faith is one of trauma and grace. Jesus's life begins in trauma—for how else can we imagine a birth for a young girl far from home? Mary's entire pregnancy must have been a traumatic event, as was the journey away from home to give birth in a backwater town, apparently without support. Jesus's earliest days are spent running from cruel Herod's despotic mania, fleeing into the land that enslaved his ancestors against the backdrop of the slaughter of the innocents that is truly one of the most horrific and vile scriptural events. When Jesus is presented in the temple, his mother learns that a sword will one day pierce her own soul. The omnipresence of the Roman empire in the lives of New Testament

---

3. Sancken, *Words That Heal*, §1722–24.

4. Hunsinger, *Bearing the Unbearable*, 14 (emphasis hers).

5. See Rambo, *Resurrecting Wounds*.

6. Keshgegian, *Redeeming Memories*, 23.

characters is a clue to the presence of colonial trauma—Jesus and his followers live amid the violence of colonial rule, made worse by their apparent poverty. The fevers, disabilities, corpses come to life—all of these point to the trauma of first century life. Jesus's death on the cross is in one sense a narrative of political trauma, a shameful and humiliating end. "At the very epicenter of Christian faith, community and practice, stands the utter traumatization of Jesus, the Christ . . . Jesus did not survive his experience of traumatic overwhelm and violence."[7] The gospel is always haunted by the cross, as a public and unimaginable public event that shaped the lives of Jesus's disciples and those who witnessed his death. "Traumatic loss lies at the very heart of the Christian imagination."[8]

The resurrection is the centerpiece of Christian good news. However, even the resurrection can be perceived as a traumatic event for Jesus's followers. The dead are supposed to stay dead, and yet suddenly the disciples were confronted with a ghost—a continuing presence that shattered their existing frameworks of life and death. Tom Troeger asks in a sermon about the Gospel of Mark, "What if death is not a reliable absolute? Then the comfort of knowing that life is a fixed and closed system is called into question. If death is overcome, if the one indestructible certitude that marks existence is shattered, then reality is wide open!"[9] It is indeed good news that reality is wide open, but the presence of continuing life where death was normative and expected is itself a traumatic event. As Jones writes, trauma is "not something outside of faith, something foreign and distant that the Christian message of grace had to struggle to address . . . parts of our rich faith traditions were born in the midst of unspeakable terrors and that grace had long been unfurling its warmth and succor therein."[10]

Trauma is thus implicated in the central narratives of our faith, as well as embedded in the sanctuary. Imagine, for a moment, what it might feel like for someone who bears on their body and soul the outcomes of violence to behold a crucifix hanging at the front of the sanctuary? In our baptismal services, we proclaim death by drowning. In the sacrament of holy communion, we glorify Christ's body and blood, and we remember the trauma of the cross. Our theology, biblical interpretation, and pastoral homiletic practices will be enhanced by contemplation of the effects of trauma and

7. Baldwin, *Trauma-Sensitive Theology*, 120.

8. Hunsinger, *Bearing the Unbearable*, 1.

9. Quoted in Jones, *Trauma and Grace*, 95–96.

10. Jones, *Trauma and Grace*, ch. 1.

the search for healing. How necessary it is to engage in such contemplation: "Left to fester on its own and without care, the wounds of trauma present in individuals, communities, and our societies will amplify and become increasingly extreme, rigid and polarized."[11] Thus, it is vital that we explore the theologies and rituals that shape our Christian practices in search of an adequate response to traumatic wounding.

Trauma-Sensitive Theology

What are the hallmarks of a trauma-sensitive theology? Jennifer Baldwin names four primary commitments of such a theology: the priority of bodily experience, full acceptance of trauma narratives, natural given-ness of human psychological multiplicity, and faith in the robust resiliency of trauma survivors.[12]

The first primary commitment of a trauma-sensitive theology is to identify trauma as fundamentally a bodily experience. Some traumatic events affect the body in obvious ways (i.e., injury, illness, or sexual abuse), but all traumatic events have somatic effects, including changes in natural hormone levels. The body cannot be ignored in responses to trauma and trauma disorders. Christian theology as a whole has been guilty of downplaying the reality of the body in preference for spirit and soul.[13] This focus on the physicality of human existence is a challenge for preaching, which aims primarily at affect and intellect and at first glance has little to do with the human body. When it comes to understanding and healing trauma, however, "you can be fully in charge of your life only if you can acknowledge the reality of your body, in all its visceral dimensions."[14] Flesh is constitutive of human life—we are dependent and interdependent because we walk around in flesh and blood. Flesh is the site of traumatic violence and wounding, and it cannot be ignored in any theology that seeks to comfort, challenge, or repair the wounds of trauma.

The second primary commitment of a trauma-sensitive theology is the acceptance of trauma narratives. Survivors often resist telling their stories because they fear they will not be believed or that their experiences will be questioned. "Survivors of traumatic interpersonal violence are especially

11. Baldwin, *Trauma-Sensitive Theology*, 157.

12. Baldwin, *Trauma-Sensitive Theology*, 7.

13. Baldwin, *Trauma-Sensitive Theology*, 8.

14. Van der Kolk, *Body Keeps Score*, 27.

vulnerable to the secondary injury of having the narratives discounted, overanalyzed, claimed as false, exaggerated or manipulative."[15] In order to provide support, pastoral professionals need to listen to narratives as they are told, understood, and experienced by survivors in the moment at which they are spoken aloud. Theology must make space for the narratives of trauma that may contradict narratives of grace and healing.

The third primary commitment is to accept the multiplicity of human psychology. Human beings are often pulled in multiple directions, creating a kind of ambivalence characterized by experiencing more than one emotion or perception at once. For example, a trauma survivor may feel anger or shame but also realize that there is more to the human person than these emotions.[16] A person experiencing trauma might find moments of hope but be unable to imagine the future as a time free from traumatic injury. While traumatic injury may lead to a person feeling broken or irreparable, they are still able to function on multiple levels. This awareness of multiplicity leads to a realization that there is room for both brokenness and resiliency. Pastoral caregivers are subject to the same types of multiplicity—they may be both horrified in the face of traumatic disclosure and also calm and able to respond in a quiet and approachable manner.

The fourth primary commitment named by Baldwin is the robust resiliency of trauma survivors. She contradicts those theorists that claim that there is no possible healing from trauma: "Trauma-sensitive theology and praxis holds resolutely and fiercely, prescriptively and descriptively to the capacity for and offering of trauma processing, recovery and resiliency required for negotiating post-traumatic response and processing."[17] This reflects a firm belief that healing is possible for many trauma survivors and that theology has a role to play in such healing and recovery. While I affirm that such healing and recovery is possible, it is difficult to know how much we can claim for the task of preaching. Do we move people toward healing, or do we merely create a space in which healing and transformation can occur? If preaching can and should play a role in healing and reconciling (to others, to God, to nature), then what is that role in the face of trauma? These are questions I will continue to explore in the remaining chapters.

These four commitments are a helpful starting point for rethinking theology in the face of trauma. In what follows, I am attempting to unpack

---

15. Baldwin, *Trauma-Sensitive Theology*, 8–9.

16. Baldwin, *Trauma-Sensitive Theology*, 9.

17. Baldwin, *Trauma-Sensitive Theology*, 10.

several more areas of theological focus that I believe will help preachers to navigate the murky waters surrounding trauma. Serene Jones argues that we must wrestle with the foundational beliefs that inspire our theological reflection:

> If the church's message about God's love for the world is to be offered to those who suffer these wounds, then we must think anew about how we use language and how we put bodies in motion and employ imagery and sound. With fresh openness we must grapple with the meaning of beliefs not only about grace, but also about such matters as sin, redemption, hope, community, communion, violence, death, crucifixion and resurrection.[18]

Preaching, Theology, and Trauma

Preaching can harm as well as heal. Baldwin notes that there are two common areas in which harm can occur in religious and theological settings. The first is "when we mistake the signs and symptoms of traumatic wounding as indicative of a lack of faith or moral fortitude."[19] This error is an easy one to make, especially in our preaching about the nature of healing and recovery. For example, the manner in which we interpret texts about faith and healing has a profound impact on those who have experienced traumatic wounding. While we might be tempted to interpret Jesus's healings as a sign of the faith of those who are healed, we must account for those who do not experience healing despite a robust faith. We must be careful not to unintentionally imply that those who do not receive healing somehow have a weak or unarticulated faith. People get sick and die, no matter how strongly they believe in Jesus. The second area in which harm can occur is when "our homiletics, teaching and liturgy unreflectively promote uses of power and social practices that contribute to sin and abuses of relational power."[20] We might promote such uses of power when we ignore the social systems that underlie certain kinds of traumatic events, or when we assume that trauma does not impact the lives of our listeners. Baldwin goes on to say that "trauma-sensitive theology seeks to mitigate the risk of theological or spiritual abuse of power by

---

18. Jones, *Trauma and Grace*, 11.
19. Baldwin, *Trauma-Sensitive Theology*, 161.
20. Baldwin, *Trauma-Sensitive Theology*, 162.

offering an alternative vision of divine power, theological anthropology, and the dynamics between sin and salvation."[21]

Preaching offers a theological language for understanding and responding to trauma. In response to trauma, preachers can choose to display a "preferential option for those who suffer and experience traumatic wounding."[22] All preachers will struggle to find good news in the face of terrible suffering. Suffering calls everything we know and everything we hope into question. Faith can help survivors on the road to recovery, but it can also harm, depending on how God is understood. "The realization that the core presuppositions of faith are inadequate in providing clarity of meaning or support in the face of traumatizing crisis events is, for many people, part of what makes traumatizing crisis events so destabilizing."[23] In other words, traumatizing crisis events interfere with the experience and interpretation of God's action in the world. If we understand God as all powerful, then we will be left with many unanswerable questions about why God appears to allow such terrible things to happen.

For preaching, theological engagement with the world is critical—it is a profoundly contextual act. Theology matters for preaching, not only with regard to the content of our preaching but also with the extent to which preaching is an act of creating theology: Homiletical theology, for example, "sees its theological task in relation to the practices and theories that serve the preaching of the gospel in contexts, cultures, and situations. It understands homiletics not as an application of theology, but a site for *doing* theology."[24] Preaching is a space of conversation among preachers and hearers, and thus a place where theology is produced.[25] The sermon itself is a space in which we wrestle with theological claims, claims that are especially unstable when placed up against the realities of trauma. Jacobsen writes that a huge gap opens up between the reading of the Scripture and the beginning of a sermon—a gap in which we are yearning for a word from the Lord—the theological high point of a Sunday morning.[26] What word will we bring to those who have suffered traumatic wounding? Homiletic theology is not a systematic task but rather a "provisional

21. Baldwin, *Trauma-Sensitive Theology*, 161–62.
22. Baldwin, *Trauma-Sensitive Theology*, 155.
23. Baldwin, *Trauma-Sensitive Theology*, 53.
24. Jacobsen, "Homiletical Theology."
25. Jacobsen, *Homiletical Theology*, 4.
26. Jacobsen, *Homiletical Theology*, 6.

and constructive enterprise."[27] We wonder how "theology can function to validate the wounding of traumatic overwhelm and take care to avoid retraumatizing survivors or engage in practices that are theologically or spiritually abusive."[28] The very notion of homiletic theology implies that we are creating theology together through the homiletic process. This provides a space of agency for the people bearing traumatic wounds, who become participants in producing theology within the sermon. In this view, preaching is "theology on the way"—our sermons both respond to more traditional theologies and participate in the creation of new theologies that respond to real human experiences of the divine. Our theologies must take into account the experience of those who have been traumatized and attempt to account for the ongoingness of traumatic wounding.

While theology is both a resource for preaching and an outcome of the preaching process, theology must be approached with care in the context of traumatic wounding if it is not to exacerbate the pain experienced by trauma survivors. This is difficult work. There are many reasons that we may fail to bear witness to trauma, insofar as we refuse "to allow the reality of violence to challenge theological accounts of God's justice, grace, sin and redemption."[29] While we may believe that God is just and redemptive, human experience may proclaim a different truth. Violence and suffering do indeed cause us to wrestle with themes of justice, grace, sin, and redemption. What follows in this section is not at all systematic but, rather, reflects on some theological commonplaces, considering some of their implications for preaching amidst trauma.

Ecclesiology

I believe that the interplay between preaching and ecclesiology is essential. Preaching participates in the ongoing conversation among God and God's people—including those who are victims of trauma. The church, as the body of Christ, is connected together—what affects one affects all. This is true of those sitting next to us in the pews, as well as those who dwell on the other side of the world whom we will never meet. Interpersonal, loving relationships are a "crucial way in which God mediates grace" to rectify

27. Jacobsen, *Homiletical Theology*, 45.

28. Baldwin, *Trauma-Sensitive Theology*, 93.

29. Hess, *Sites of Violence*, 105.

traumatic wounding.[30] In the church we have an opportunity to encounter and enact such loving relationships. It is an act of self-giving love to witness to the trauma experienced by others.

The church, as a body, cannot be complete without making space for the experiences of others—the very identity of one is unthinkable without the others.[31] Miroslav Volf determines that we must enlarge our thinking "by letting the voices and perspectives of others, especially those with whom we may be in conflict, resonate within ourselves, by allowing them to help us see them, as well as ourselves, from *their* perspective, and if needed readjust our perspectives as we take into account their perspectives."[32] This is how the church must proceed to think theologically in the face of trauma—by allowing the perspectives of others, especially those who have experienced wounding, to shape our communal theologies.

Sadly, the church has also been a perpetrator of trauma.[33] Sexual abuse and misconduct by church leaders has been a reality in far too many contexts. In my Canadian context, churches joined with the government to participate in centuries of marginalization of Indigenous peoples. The modern church in particular participated in colonialism and imperialism, leading to the traumatization of whole populations. While it is difficult to know how such harm can be mitigated, sermons become a place for acknowledgment and confession of these sins.

The Doctrine of God and the Doctrine of the Trinity

While it is possible to know God intimately, it is impossible to say anything about God that is complete or unlimited. God is a God beyond our knowing, and it is only through our imaginative viewing of divine revelation that we can say anything at all. In the face of trauma, it matters how we construct a vision of God. Baldwin believes that there are two areas of "God talk" that are most central to a trauma-sensitive theology—one is divine relationality and the other is divine power.[34]

---

30. Beste, *God and the Victim*, 14.

31. Volf, *Exclusion and Embrace*, 158.

32. Volf, *Exclusion and Embrace*, 213.

33. See Sancken, *Words that Heal*, ch. 3, for an excellent discussion of the manner in which churches have been perpetrators of violence and suffering.

34. Baldwin, *Trauma-Sensitive Theology*, 98.

I believe that traumatic wounding is best addressed by a vision of God who is powerful but not dominating, who honors difference and multiplicity and is self-giving. The Social Doctrine of the Trinity provides such a resource, as a "vision of cohesive multiplicity in optimal relationality."[35] The persons of the Trinity live in intimate relation to one another—and the suffering of one contributes to the suffering of all. To image God in such a way provides a way to imagine right relationships among the human community. While we can only mirror God's nature in some respects, the love and self-giving of the Trinity offers a template for how we might respond to each other in the face of trauma. We can imagine a perichoretic space at the very center of God in which there is room for redemptive community to emerge. Here the Holy Spirit acts as a gracious and undefined presence. When our human words and prayers fail, the Spirit intercedes with a language that is beyond our knowing: "Likewise the Spirit helps us in our weakness; for we do not know how to pray as we ought, but that very Spirit intercedes with sighs too deep for words."[36]

One of the most common well-meaning yet misguided statements that people make following a trauma is "It was God's will." In a sermon following the death of his son in a motor vehicle accident, William Sloane Coffin Jr. preached these words: "Nothing so infuriates me as the incapacity of seemingly intelligent people to get it through their heads that God doesn't go around this world with his finger on triggers, his fist around knives, his hands on steering wheels. God is dead set against all unnatural deaths."[37] While we do not wish to deny that God is powerful, it is harmful to assume that God has willed traumatic events, which posits God as "the supreme perpetrator of trauma and violence."[38] It is preferable to craft a vision of God in which the divine suffers with humanity, sheds the first tear, and grieves trauma as much as we do.

Soteriology and Theological Anthropology

Shelley Rambo has argued that "trauma is the key to articulating a theology of redemption rather than the problem around which theology must

---

35. Baldwin, *Trauma-Sensitive Theology*, 99.

36. Rom 8:26 NRSV.

37. Coffin, "Alex's Death" in Bush, *This Incomplete One*, 55–50 (57).

38. Baldwin, *Trauma-Sensitive Theology*, 101.

navigate."[39] The lens of trauma casts a different light on the nature of life and death, sin and salvation.

How do we deal with the problem of sin in relation to trauma? While there may be a relationship between sin and certain kinds of illness, in general sin cannot account for illness. It is a different matter when we consider the ways that human beings treat each other. Baldwin claims that sin, rather than a natural state of humanity, is an abuse of relational power.[40] She writes, "This definition includes the use of systematic, social, interpersonal, or intrapersonal power in a manner that reduces or leads to the 'absence of well-being' in self, others, society or the ecological world."[41] Sin, then, is about human relationships. If we view sin through the lens of human relationships, salvation becomes about "healing, soothing and unburdening the wounds and beliefs consequent to sinful abuses of relational power, including those that reach the degree of traumatic overwhelm and those that remain below the threshold."[42] We preach to victims and perpetrators of trauma. While we must take sides and honor the experience of the victim, we must also make space for the healing and recovery of those who have caused trauma to others.

There are a variety of ways that theology has understood salvation and the manner in which Jesus Christ leads to salvation. Whether one embraces satisfaction, Christus victor, moral influence, or another theory of atonement, it is important to think through how these theories relate to the problem of trauma. A problem with all of these theories is that they valorize suffering and death, a perspective that Baldwin names as dangerous in the face of trauma: "traumatic overwhelm, suffering and death are not a means to a good."[43] In this sense, suffering itself is not redemptive. At best, the traumatizing death of Jesus makes space for the possibility that God suffers with humanity, that God comprehends the depth and terror of grief suffered by so many in our world.

Jennifer Beste approaches human and divine relationships from the perspective of trauma and feminist theory, wondering if there really is nothing that can separate human beings from God's grace given the realities of

---

39. Rambo, *Spirit and Trauma*, 11.

40. Baldwin, *Trauma-Sensitive Theology*, 113.

41. Baldwin, *Trauma-Sensitive Theology*, 115.

42. Baldwin, *Trauma-Sensitive Theology*, 127.

43. Baldwin, *Trauma-Sensitive Theology*, 132.

trauma and interpersonal violence.[44] In other words, are human beings really free to respond to God's grace in the face of trauma? Beste acknowledges that "interpersonal harm has the power to destroy a person's capacity to realize sufficient freedom to love self, neighbor, and God."[45] What is the nature of human freedom when we are accosted by events and situations that lie outside our capacity to cope? What is the nature of human freedom when we face life-threatening illness?

The question of human suffering is at the center of a theological response to trauma. Human beings have always wondered how a good, omnipotent God could allow such terrible things to happen in the world. Some of what happens in the world can be attributed to human sin—physical and sexual abuse are clear examples, as is gun violence. Other calamities are less easy to categorize. What do we believe about the causes of natural disasters or pandemics? Tom Long, in his book *What Shall We Say?*, seeks to "stand with preachers, who then will stand with their parishioners, in thinking through how faith in a loving God holds together with the facts of life in a suffering world."[46] This seems like an impossible task for most preachers—these are unanswerable questions and unsolvable problems, especially in light of trauma. There are some potential answers that are likely more harmful than others. For example, we might blame the victim for their own suffering. We might fail to witness to the suffering at all—preferring to ignore or supress it. We might advocate a "ministry of presence" that fails to attend to the structural and political underpinnings of violence in our culture.

Guilt can be an outcome of suffering, especially in relation to traumatic wounding, in which case individuals may struggle with their actions, or failures to act, blaming themselves for the outcomes of the traumatic event. "Traumatized people struggle to arrive at a fair and reasonable assessment of their conduct, finding a balance between unrealistic guilt and denial of all moral responsibility."[47] Preachers should avoid any tendency to blame the victim, especially in our conversations about sin. At the same time, survivors may need to hear an assurance of pardon—that there is nothing they can do to make God love them more, and nothing they can do to make God love them less.

44. See Beste, *God and the Victim*.

45. Beste, *God and the Victim*, 14.

46. Long, *What Shall We Say?*, xiii.

47. Herman, *Trauma and Recovery*, 68.

Eschatology and Hope

Tiffany Thomas is a pastor who preached through four national tragedies in her first few years as a pastoral minister. She writes,

> There is only one word to describe preaching after the recurring violence that is shaking the nation: traumatic. It is a trauma for the nation, for the Christian community, and for the pastor. We ask ourselves: *How am I going to do this again? And again? Why does this keep happening?*
>
> In moments like these, preaching is not glamorous or fun. Preaching is painful. It's painful because in moments like these, a preacher very clearly feels her limitations. She is ill-equipped to provide the right words. There are not enough words in the English language to make sense of something so senseless. She is also limited in that she needs to hear hope as much as those she has been called on to express hope. And yet the task to articulate hope in the midst of darkness remains before her.[48]

Articulating hope is an essential task of preaching, and yet many individuals and communities who face trauma may find it difficult to be hopeful. As Thomas notes, we are confronted with our own limitations as preachers when we are called upon to preach hope in terrible circumstances. Preachers must draw on theological resources in order to begin to find a way forward.

Christian theology places tremendous importance on the "not yet." We have a vision of God's future as a time in which full healing and wholeness can be found—something that the whole creation waits for with eager longing. However, it can be too easy to relegate the hope of healing to a far distant day. There is a danger that we ignore the real-time suffering of bodies and minds, as one of the commitments of trauma-sensitive theology is to pay attention to the importance of the body.

After my son died at the age of three, an acquaintance sent a beautiful note with the words "we are all born for heaven." I found these words comforting—after all, there is grace in the idea that my son is now safe with God. There is, however, a double-edged sword here. I was traumatized not only by his death after a long illness but also by the absence of his body. As any mother knows, the actual physical bodies of our children matter. While I wanted to believe, struggled to believe, that I would hold him again one day, it was the gut-wrenchingly painful absence that mattered in

---

48. Thomas, "Preaching in the Midst of Tragedy."

the depths of grief. It can be dangerous when we attempt to override grief and present struggle with a distant and seemingly impossible hope. In the words of Nicholas Wolterstorff in the foreword to a book of sermons from the funerals of children, "Though grief does not smother hope, neither does hope smother grief."[49]

Theology of the Cross

It is impossible to write about trauma, suffering, and transformation without considering the theology of the cross. In the twentieth century, the theology of the cross underwent significant critiques and challenges, "raising the question of whether the cross was a symbol of redemption or whether it is a symbol that needed to be redeemed."[50] On one hand, the cross is at the center of Christian theology, as a symbol of God's decision to suffer with, and on behalf of, humanity. Christians have always interpreted their suffering through the suffering of Jesus. The cross can be a helpful theological resource for supporting those who have suffered: "The cross, as a symbol of Jesus's suffering, forces Christians to confront their own traumatic experiences, their loss and grief and the suffering that ensues . . . The symbol of the cross and the story behind it can provide hope, assuring the trauma survivor that he is not alone, that God also suffers and that he is surrounded by a community of those who suffer."[51]

On the other hand, the cross has been used as a triumphalistic symbol of glory. Douglas John Hall defines *triumphalism* as "the tendency in all strongly held worldviews, whether religious or secular, to present themselves as full and complete accounts of reality, leaving little if any room for debate or difference of opinion and expecting of their adherents unflinching belief and loyalty."[52] Oftentimes, our interpretations of the cross are triumphalist, presenting it as a final and complete account of reality. When it is used as a symbol that announces the complete victory of life over death, the cross may not leave room for experiences of death and violent wounding that defy any easy grace. In reality, what continues after death is somehow less triumphant.[53] If we interpret Christ's words on the cross, "It is finished,"

49. "Foreword" in Bush, *Incomplete One*, x.

50. Rambo, *Resurrecting Wounds*, 6.

51. Rendon, *Upside*, §1988.

52. Hall, *Cross in Our Context*, 17.

53. Rambo, *Resurrecting Wounds*, 2.

to imply that there is no further suffering or death or woundedness after the cross, then we are ignoring and inverting the experiences of those who continue to suffer. "How, *in this world of the here and now*, are we to perceive the presence of the crucified one . . . ?"[54] If the question of redemption is intended for this world and not only some far off distant eschaton, then how might we conceive of the cross? The cross announces death as a real thing—there is no sugar-coating the violence and suffering that Jesus experienced on the cross. It proclaims the reality of human capacity to harm others—Jesus was hung on an imperial cross.

Rambo writes that it is critical to think not only about the cross but also life after the cross. "The return of unintegrated suffering as narrated in trauma not only sheds light on how we make sense of recurring, intrusive symptoms and the re-emergence of forms of oppression, such as racism and sexism; but also it presents an invitation to reconceive the story that we tell about life in the aftermath of the cross—the story of resurrection."[55] She argues that the return of Jesus witnesses to life in the midst of death—where death and life are coterminous and intermingled. How might we think of resurrection in light of the ongoingness of trauma? Rambo turns to the gospel of John, and the story that is traditionally referred to as "Doubting Thomas." In this gospel account, Jesus appears to his disciples in the Upper Room. This is his second appearance to them—Thomas missed the first one, and is no doubt struggling to integrate all that his friends have conveyed to him. This time, Thomas is also a witness to the resurrection. Thomas is invited to come close to Jesus, to touch his wounds. We don't know whether Thomas touches or not—but the presence of the risen Christ in some way provides the evidence he needs, and he proclaims, "My Lord and my God." Rambo argues that the presence of the wounds is highly significant for interpreting this narrative. The struggle of the disciples to see to recognize Jesus is also significant "and underscores how difficult it is to resurrect, to come to life again."[56] The resurrection is central to Christian faith, and yet in the face of trauma it is useful to read these gospel narratives afresh as a way of recognizing the returning wounds that figure on the body of Jesus. This is not a pure, unblemished, shining body, but a body that portrays the reality of bodily suffering on the cross. We cannot talk about resurrection unless we also talk about wounds.

54. Hall, *Cross in Our Context*, 42.
55. Rambo, *Resurrecting Wounds*, 6–7.
56. Rambo, *Resurrecting Wounds*, 9.

Theology of the Gospel

Theology begins with a wound.[57] In the words of David Jacobsen, "If the central task of homiletical theology, and the practice of preaching that embodies its theological task, is the naming of the gospel, this work is done not in some once-and-for-all state, but with the complications, secondary infections, and scars as they emerge over time."[58] The task of naming gospel amid the woundedness of trauma is an ongoing and complex process. We articulate the gospel not as a once-and-for-all but amidst the contours of real life.

One of the central questions of this book is "What is gospel in relation to trauma?" Along with Serene Jones, I affirm that we should proclaim grace. But how?[59] It seems that gospel should be straightforward—simply the good news that Jesus died and rose again for the salvation of the world (however one might define salvation). It is gospel that God acts in the world, that God loves, that God has imagined a future for us that is in many ways beyond our own imagining. Gospel, however, at least when it comes to trauma, is more complicated. Gospel is not a fixed and unchanging entity but unfolds in a particular historical context. I would argue that trauma is one of those contexts in which gospel is unfolded and interpreted. We must measure our definitions of gospel against the ongoingness of trauma. Thus, what is gospel or good news will depend on the context. It is an act of theological reflection to name gospel. It may be that traumatic events and their aftermath require new namings of good news that may or may not coincide with more general understandings of gospel. What is life, power, promise in the face of trauma?

Paul Scott Wilson is the originator of one of the most popular models for biblical preaching—*The Four Pages of the Sermon*.[60] It is a fully articulated and theologically sound treatment of trouble and grace for preaching, emerging from a law/gospel homiletical school.[61] Wilson names four theological functions that are to be articulated on "four pages" of a sermon: Trouble in the Bible, trouble in the world, God's action in the Bible, God's action in the world. Trouble is the sin, which often puts the burden on

57. Fulkerson, *Places of Redemption*, 12.

58. Jacobsen, "Gospel as Transfiguring Promise," 138.

59. Jones, *Trauma and Grace*, 12.

60. Wilson, *Four Pages of the Sermon*.

61. Wilson, *Preaching and Homiletical Theory*, 91.

humanity to act differently. Grace, on the other hand, is a free act of God that takes the burden away from humanity.

A focus on God's action is a strength of Wilson's model, but one of the realities of trouble is that it is sometimes hard to see what God is doing—in fact, trauma victims often wonder if God is doing anything at all. We must somehow account for those times when God is silent or when divine action is difficult to discern. It is also easy to misinterpret what God is doing—in fact, in the face of an omnipotent God it might be tempting to blame God for what has happened. One can imagine this to be especially true in situations in which natural disaster or "act of God" causes the trauma or, for example, when the perpetrator of abuse is a trusted representative of the church.

Both the balancing of trouble and grace and the naming of grace become difficult in the face of trauma. The trouble is clear—wounding of the body and soul, whether by illness, fear, or violence, constitutes trouble in both the text and the world. The grace may be less clear. Wilson perceives that trouble and grace are two poles, which, when brought into proximity, spark a particular tension—a spark of imagination. This spark is a third entity that produces a tensive event in which the interpreter participates.[62] "By juxtaposing trouble and grace, and by the power of the Holy Spirit, a third identity is generated, an identity of faith, hope, and love of God and neighbor. The result is far from a static modern notion of polar opposites; it is a generative postmodern tension that momentarily resists deconstructive tendencies in favor of a strong claim on behalf of God."[63] While this generative tension holds promise for the way we think about gospel and preaching, Wilson's model does not fully account for the dilemma of getting from trouble to grace in the face of trauma. Wilson to some extent allows for this ambiguity: "The gospel does not make everything 'all better,' but it does put things in appropriate perspective before a loving and redeeming God who rules over all. When we tell stories of God's action, we are telling stories from the perspective of faith, and ambiguity in the outcome should not be removed."[64] In addition, "Page Four does not erase Page Two, and does not suggest 'happily ever after,' but it sounds a strong alternative note of grace in the midst of passing life."[65] By all means, it is valuable to sound

62. Wilson, *Preaching and Homiletical Theory*, 92.

63. Wilson, *Preaching and Homiletical Theory*, 99.

64. Wilson, *Four Pages of the Sermon*, 221.

65. Wilson, *Four Pages of the Sermon*, 203.

an alternative note of grace that can resist or challenge the powers of sin and death that lead to traumatic wounding, but we still have to wrestle with the manner in which we claim God acts in the world, especially for those who feel that God is doing nothing at all. In the strange in-betweenness of trauma, life and death intermingle in indeterminant ways. In Rambo's understanding of what remains, life does not erase the woundedness of death. She calls us to resist the "triumphalistic linear progression from death to life."[66] In that sense, trouble does not give way to grace. Instead, grace intermingles with trouble. In the words of Flora Keshgegian, "Theologically, the redemptive potential of the memory of Jesus Christ will in no small measure be known and realized by the capacity of that memory to hold and carry not only the story of Jesus, but the stories of all those who suffer, struggle, live and die."[67] Thus, I am arguing that the space between trouble and grace, the space between page two and page four, must be taken seriously as a space in which trouble and grace intermingle. The easy movement between trouble and grace in this model of preaching implies that we too move easily between the two, and that is not always the case, especially with regard to traumatic wounding.

Getting to the Gospel Too Soon

The rock opera *Jesus Christ Superstar* was widely criticized when it debuted in 1970.[68] It was seen as sacrilegious by many, at least in part because it ends with crucifixion, not resurrection. "Many Christians see this as a critical component of the story, one that if removed alters the entire narrative. In fact, the Apostle Paul himself wrote in his first epistle to the Corinthians, 'And if Christ has not been raised, our preaching is useless and so is your faith.'"[69] *Jesus Christ Superstar* never gets as far as the resurrection, but this might be an appropriate image for the ongoingness of death in the mist of life that is experienced by some trauma survivors. The death is much more present than the life that follows. As I noted at the beginning of this chapter, preachers may experience an inner pull toward the resurrection, without stopping to witness the death that remains.

---

66. Rambo, "Theologians Engaging Trauma," 227.

67. Keshgegian, *Redeeming Memories*, 31.

68. Merritt, "Glorious Glitter Bomb."

69. Merritt, "Glorious Glitter Bomb."

Rambo identifies a "public uneasiness with trauma and the push to move beyond it—an impatience with suffering, revealing a timeline on public attention and sympathy."[70] It does sometimes appear that there is a public expectation about the timeline of grief. Once upon a time, family members wore black for a specified amount of time in order to convey publicly that they were in a state of grieving. When I was once in the grasp of terrible grief, I recall wishing that such social laws were still in effect, so that those around me could be reminded in a concrete way that my grief was not yet finished. These social conventions allowed for a common understanding that grieving takes time. Of course, there are types of grief that are not measurable by public standards—grief and trauma that are socially invisible or unacceptable. For example, how does one mourn a private and personal wound such as abuse in public? Some grief, some wounds are private and buried deep within the individual. In subtle and not-so-subtle ways, we communicate an expectation that there is an appropriate amount of time to complete the grieving process—usually about a year. "There is a push to move beyond trauma . . . and a church that does not provide a space for traumatized persons to bring their experience of 'a sadness that does not go away.'"[71] There is a danger, then, that we will seek "to proclaim the good news before its time."[72] In the example of New Orleans, Rambo notes,

> there is a lot of pressure to claim that New Orleans has recovered from Katrina. There is pressure to get on with it, to move to a happy ending. He tells us about the local government's frenzy to tear down buildings. There is a hunger to remove not only traces of the storm but the pre-storm realities. In the post-storm push for fresh starts, previous forms of life are threatened. The pressure to get over, to forget, to wipe away the past, is often reinforced by one particular way of reading Christian redemption. The narrative of triumphant resurrection can often operate in such a way as to promise a radically new beginning to those who have experienced a devastating event.[73]

This use of redemptive narratives can be perceived as a push to "get over it," or "move on." In the aftermath of trauma, the boundary between life

70. Rambo, *Spirit and Trauma*, 2.

71. Rambo, *Spirit and Trauma*, 2.

72. Rambo, *Spirit and Trauma*, 3.

73. Rambo, *Spirit and Trauma*, 143.

and death is erased.[74] Rambo claims that trauma disrupts our basic narratives about life and death and has profound implications for the manner in which we construct the concept of resurrection. She seeks a narrative of redemption that can account for traumatic suffering and to retain the profound sense of God's presence, but claims

> this picture of redemption cannot emerge by interpreting death and life in opposition to each other. Instead, theology must account for the excess, or remainder, of death in life that is central to trauma. This reconfiguration of death and life, viewed through the lens of trauma, unearths a distinctive theology that can witness the realities of the aftermath of trauma.[75]

The space between life and death is complex. New life does not necessarily erase the wounds of the old; in fact, those wounds remain open. Those who survive traumatic events cannot retrieve the life they once knew, but they also cannot envision new life.[76] Traumatic events can intrude continually in the present. Rambo insists that it is vital to account theologically for "what remains."[77]

When resurrection is interpreted as a grand and final form of redemption, it fails to account for the trauma and suffering that remain even beyond the empty tomb. Rambo acknowledges that interpreting the resurrection in this way contains within it a sense of promise and hope, but it can also "gloss over difficulty, casting it within a larger framework in which the new replaces the old, and in which good inevitably wins out over evil. Death is concluded and new life is ushered in."[78] The cry of forsakenness cannot be drowned out entirely by the Alleluia's of Easter Sunday. "When we quickly move towards the celebration of what is to come which remains unknown to those living through that Friday and Saturday, we diminish the full impact of traumatic disruption and risk adding to the feelings of isolation and abandonment."[79] If we understand redemption as a sweeping and final triumph of good over evil, or a decisive and discontinuous event, then we risk ignoring or undermining the reality that trauma does not go away.

---

74. Rambo, *Spirit and Trauma*, 3.

75. Rambo, *Spirit and Trauma*, 6.

76. Rambo, *Spirit and Trauma*, 7.

77. Rambo, *Spirit and Trauma*.

78. Rambo, *Spirit and Trauma*, 6.

79. Baldwin, *Trauma-Sensitive Theology*, 121.

A theology of Holy Saturday may provide some guidance here. It takes seriously the three-day narrative of the crucifixion-resurrection event, arguing that there was a day in between Friday and Sunday in which God stayed silent and was absent. At the center of the drama of death and resurrection is an empty space in which God is hidden. This hiddenness of God may be an ongoing reality for sufferers of trauma.[80] Alan Lewis writes that this time is "only a time of waiting, in which nothing of significance occurs and of which there is little to be said."[81] We as preachers would do well to leave a space in which there is little to be said, to acknowledge a time of waiting that occurs after the trauma and before the redemption (assuming that there is eventually redemption). Teitje suggests that on Holy Saturday "our trauma, soul wounds and god-forsakenness too are brought into the very heart of Christ."[82] The silence of Holy Saturday leaves room for our own unfinished endings. We are not alone in the silence. A good example lies in our Good Friday liturgies, which often end in silence—it is the only immediate response to the trauma of the cross. Yet our silence exists in a hopeful space—we await Easter.

So how then might we understand redemption? This is an unresolved Alleluia. Time does not heal all wounds. Neither does resurrection heal all wounds. Scars and wounds persist post-resurrection—the pain does not go away. Scars and wounds "function as a means of identification as well as a symbol of the capacity for recovery and the healing over without erasure of wounds."[83] This reality is especially relevant when we are preaching scriptural texts about healing. "The vision of healing and miracles set out in the Christian gospels can be 'bad news' for those whose bodies do not conform to social norms."[84] Healing does not necessarily mean perfection and wholeness. The natural effects of aging, disability cannot be reversed. Not everyone heals from illness. This is not necessarily calling for us to preach only toward psychological and spiritual well-being—God heals bodies too—but we cannot claim that wholeness and perfection are the only kinds of healing brought on by "true faith."

What does this mean for preaching, especially as we are urged to move so quickly between trouble and grace? This kind of preaching seems to

---

80. Teitje, *Holy Saturday*, 96.

81. Lewis, *Between Cross and Resurrection*, 1.

82. Lewis, *Between Cross and Resurrection*, 94.

83. Baldwin, *Trauma-Sensitive Theology*, 137.

84. Rambo, *Resurrecting Wounds*, 63.

require a "not yet," a willingness to remain in a Holy Saturday kind of frame. In a culture of instant gratification, the "not yet" seems almost intolerable, and yet we must account, somehow, for what remains—the haunting of death that persists even amidst the possibility of new life. Where does the sacred story meet the story of suffering that is so real and present for those who have experienced trauma? How do we account for the ongoingness of death in the midst of life?[85] What is our responsibility as preachers to address the theological complexity of suffering, to resist easy transitions from death to life, leaving space in the dialogue about how new life comes about? Lives can be destroyed in an instant. Resurrection may happen more slowly. While we believe that life always prevails, it does not come immediately, at least not in all circumstances. Life does not return in any pure form—the marks of death remain.[86] Rather than triumph, says Rambo, redemption becomes about discerning life taking shape, discerning the presence of the Spirit.[87] The Spirit witnesses to death's remaining and love's survival.[88] "In the aftermath of a traumatic event, practices and ways of life that people knew before trauma can never be fully recovered and restored as they once were. Instead, forms of life must now emerge with death as a shaping force."[89] Love persists, but it is "tenuous and perilous."[90] There is a provisionality of the gospel,[91] just as wounds are, hopefully, provisional.

Elsewhere, I have written about a perichoretic space that exists at the heart of the Trinity.[92] In the space between Creator, Spirit, and Son, there emerges the possibility of communal life that is characterized by freedom, mutual self-giving, the embrace of difference, and systems that are open to change instead of closed. In this space, we are invited to live between trouble and grace, despair and hope, death and resurrection. This is a liminal space that is not one thing or the other—it is a third space between death and resurrection. We are invited to dwell in this space. "Recovery occurs in a kind of space between, not dissimilar in some ways to the space where proclamation itself occurs, a space between the active agency of preachers and

---

85. Rambo, *Spirit and Trauma*, 3.

86. Rambo, *Resurrecting Wounds*, 5.

87. Rambo, *Spirit and Trauma*, 151.

88. Rambo, *Spirit and Trauma*, 160.

89. Rambo, *Spirit and Trauma*, 162.

90. Rambo, *Spirit and Trauma*, 172

91. Jacobsen, "Gospel as Transfiguring Promise," 152.

92. Travis, *Decolonizing Preaching*, ch. 3.

listeners where control is both exercised and surrendered and the Holy Spirit brings life."[93] Keshgegian writes about the necessity of the church cultivating an epistemology of ambiguity.[94] The church's insistence on "certainty and absoluteness of truth has created the kind of social and political space for the forces of domination to enter and establish themselves."[95] This entails a willingness to critique the theologies and central narratives of the faith in light of the human experience of traumatic wounding.

Jones also perceives such a space: "In both the story of the passion and the 'trauma drama' it lives instead in a kind of third space—the space between the given and the imagined, between history and story, between event and dream. And because of this, both stories recognize that poetry rather than straightforward taletelling is often the best way to capture meaning."[96] In music, a contrapuntal is a piece of music that has two distinct melodic lines. Perhaps this is a way to think about telling the story of the resurrection in the face of trauma. We tell two stories at the same time: one of a resurrection that has overcome death, and one that testifies to the ongoingness of death even in the face of the resurrection. Sometimes our stories end raggedly, without being wrapped up with a smart and tidy bow.

The reader may be wondering what all this means in practice. Do we literally leave a space in the middle of our sermons? Do we end in silence like *Jesus Christ Superstar* without getting to resurrection? I was trained to believe that every sermon must preach the gospel. That remains true. However, as I have argued in this chapter, gospel must take into account both the wound and the healing—death and resurrection are both essential aspects of gospel. The next chapter turns to more practical ways of preaching in between, dealing with the idea of the preacher as witness.

93. Sancken, "Words Fail Us," 124.

94. Keshgegian, *Redeeming Memories*, 227.

95. Keshgegian, *Redeeming Memories*, 227.

96. Jones, *Trauma and Grace*, 79.

3

Preaching In Between: Witnessing to Trauma

C anada has participated in a national process of Truth and Reconciliation that was similar in nature to South Africa's process following Apartheid. Canada's process addressed the systematic oppression of indigenous peoples, and survivors of residential schools were invited to tell their stories. They were given intentional space to bear witness to what had happened to them at the hands of the Canadian government and churches. The introduction to the report reads, "Survivors speak of their pain, loneliness, and suffering, and of their accomplishments. While this is a difficult story, it is also a story of courage and endurance. The first step in any process of national reconciliation requires us all to attend to these voices, which have been silenced for far too long."[1] When she was less than five years old, Lynda Pahpasay McDonald was taken by plane from her home:

> I looked outside, my mom was, you know, ailing her arms, and, and I, and she must have been crying, and I see my dad grabbing her, and, I was wondering why, why my mom was, you know, she was struggling. She told me many years later what happened, and she explained to me why we had to be sent away to, to residential school. And, and I just couldn't get that memory out of my head, and I still remember to this day what, what happened that day. And she told me, like, she was so hurt, and, and I used to ask her, "Why did you let us go, like, why didn't you stop them, you know? Why didn't you, you know, come and get us?" And she told me, "We couldn't, because they told us if we tried to do anything, like,

---

1. The Truth and Reconciliation Commission of Canada, "Survivors Speak."

get you guys back, we'd be thrown into jail." So, they didn't want to end up in jail, 'cause they still had babies at, at the cabin.[2]

One can only imagine the effect of such an experience on a young girl. Thousands of children like Lynda were taken from their homes in similar circumstances, resulting in painful traumatic losses for children, families, and communities. As processes of Truth and Reconciliation recognize, in the aftermath of trauma it is vital to give space to survivors to tell their stories. Telling stories is a powerful tool. Putting traumatic memories into words is a way to ease their power, to tell the struggle out loud, and to name before others the pain that has been experienced. This chapter examines the concept of witnessing to trauma from a theological and homiletical point of view. Herman defines the study of trauma itself as "bearing witness" to the terrible events of trauma.[3] How do we witness to the power of trauma in both personal and collective contexts while also witnessing to a larger story of grace and mercy that is found in the gospel?

Witness

What does it mean to witness? The term *martyr*, which is the Greek for *witness*, commonly refers to one who sacrifices—sometimes, a witness is one who dies because of what they have seen and what they say about it. To witness can be literally to see events take place—as we witness a crime, or a car accident, or, positively, the birth of a child. In the case of violence and violation, Kaethe Weingarten has coined the term *common shock*; *common* because it affects everyone, it is collective.[4] Common shock is "triggered by our being witness to an event or an interaction that we appraise as disturbing,"[5] with PTSD being an extreme reaction. While the experience of witnessing an ethnic slur aimed at another person differs in comparison to being the target of such a slur, it is important to honor all these experiences as ones that lead to this common shock.[6] The witness occupies a particular position in relation to two other roles: victim

---

2. The Truth and Reconciliation Commission of Canada, "Survivors Speak."

3. Herman, *Trauma and Recovery*, 7.

4. Weingarten, *Common Shock*, 6.

5. Weingarten, *Common Shock*, 9.

6. Weingarten, *Common Shock*, 14.

and perpetrator.[7] The witness observes something happening to someone else—they may be present at the time of the interaction, or hear about it afterwards. Rambo offers the following observation: "By definition, a witness is an observer, an onlooker, a bystander, or a spectator of a particular event or events. The juridical use of the term adds another dimension to this; the observer is also called upon to speak about the events—to testify or bear witness on behalf of someone or something."[8] Sometimes, we give voice to what we have seen and experienced—we bear witness—describing as best we can what we have seen, as a witness does in a courtroom drama. We may also bear witness to what has been done to us—telling our own stories about our experience. Literature and other forms of art bear witness to experiences and stories—in a variety of genres, they give shape to the narratives that define our lives.

Witness studies is a thriving intellectual art that seeks to understand exactly what happens when we witness, or bear witness to, events and experiences. In a courtroom, the hope is that witnesses will be able to testify to the facts, what actually happened. Studies from social psychology, however, tell us that witnesses are often unreliable, even when they believe they are telling the truth. Many variables impact our memories of events, meaning that sometimes we are unable to reconstruct or narrate events exactly as they have taken place. Trauma particularly impairs the natural functions of the body and mind, interfering with memory and recall. "As a relation to events, testimony seems to be composed of bits and pieces of a memory that has been overwhelmed by occurrences that have not settled into understanding or remembrance, acts that cannot be construed as knowledge nor assimilated into full cognition."[9] A trauma survivor may or may not be able to bear witness to the events and experiences that caused the trauma in the first place. They benefit tremendously, however, when they are able to testify to their own experience with a compassionate and generous listener.

What does it mean to tell the truth in difficult circumstances such as the aftermath of trauma? In the face of trauma and unbearable events such as the Holocaust and other genocides, we need to wrestle with the concept of witness. While we might think of a witness as a passive participant in an event, witnessing is actually a deeper and more significant action in that the witness is intimately affected by what they have witnessed. What we see

7. Weingarten, *Common Shock*, 22.

8. Rambo, *Spirit and Trauma*, 38.

9. Felman, "Education and Crisis," 16.

changes us in small and large ways, and we can never go back to be the person we were before we witnessed the event. In the case of traumatic events, the witness may feel guilt, fear, shock, anger, a sense of helplessness, even relief if they were not hurt or directly involved. Kaethe Weingarten tells a story about a young woman who witnessed the chaos and devastation as the planes hit the twin towers on September 11, 2001. The woman said, "I don't know why I feel so bad. After all, nothing happened to me!"[10] However, something did happen to this woman—"she was an unwilling witness to horror, death and destruction."[11] To witness trauma is "to have something happen to us."[12] Another example arises from the situation of COVID-19, the pandemic that swept the globe in 2020. As we witnessed the devastating spread of the illness, we all lived through the fear of getting sick. We witnessed the pandemic, but we participated in it as well.

Theologically, a witness is one who sees what God is doing and may be compelled to name out loud what they have seen and experienced. Jesus offers the great promise in Acts: "you will receive power when the Holy Spirit has come upon you; and you will be my witnesses in Jerusalem, in all Judea and Samaria, and to the ends of the earth."[13] The Holy Spirit enables the followers of Jesus to go out into the world and tell a story about what they have seen and experienced in relation to Jesus's life and ministry. This task is continued by the church today as it bears witness to the presence and power of the Triune God. Preachers are also witnesses—to the experience of God acting in the world, to the experiences and occurrences that shape our own daily lives and those of others.

Thomas Long views witnessing to the gospel as the organizing and governing principle of the whole process of preaching.[14] He argues that the concept of *witness* has not been more present in homiletic literature because it is often associated with a fairly aggressive form of evangelism and also because preachers may be uncomfortable with the legal associations of the term.[15] Long views the term *witness* as valuable for preaching because it emphasizes the authority of the preacher as one who has "seen and heard"—they have encountered God in some way during the

---

10. Weingarten, *Common Shock*, 39.

11. Weingarten, *Common Shock*, 39.

12. Weingarten, *Common Shock*, 39.

13. Acts 1:8 NRSV.

14. Long, *Witness of Preaching*, ix.

15. Long, *Witness of Preaching*, 46–47.

process of preparing and delivering a sermon, through the Scriptures.[16] Those who witness God's action in the Scriptures must find a way to articulate—to verbalize—those encounters, telling the story in a way that honors both the literary form of the text and the experience of the preacher herself.[17] The witness is always involved in the testimony but not as a neutral observer. The preacher stands with a particular community of faith, participates "in the mission of a specific community of faith, goes to the Scripture on behalf of that community, and hears a particular word for them on this day and in this place."[18]

Anna Carter Florence names testimony as passionate truth-telling.[19] She draws on a traditional definition of *testimony* as "both a narration of events and a confession of belief: we tell what we have seen and heard, and we confess what we believe about it."[20] Preachers are ones who see, and ones who speak.

Preachers are witnesses to trauma in a number of ways. Firstly, we literally see trauma as it occurs within our own circle of influence and at a wider cultural level. We see it as bystanders and as participants—sometimes we are the ones who are traumatized, sometimes we merely stand by and watch as others suffer (not because we don't want to act, but because we don't know what can or should be done). Pastorally, we often sit with those who suffer and hear firsthand the stories that have come to define and shape their lives. We have the poignant task of "hearing one another to speech," when we listen carefully and allow trauma to be spoken out loud.[21]

Secondly, we are invited to testify to the reality of traumatic harm that occurs in our culture and in our pews—to bear witness. The pulpit is a space in which trauma can be named and remembered. It is a place that belongs to a community, where stories can be told that break patterns of alienation and loneliness. It is representative of a web of relationships, between preacher and listener and among listeners, and may even stand in for the relationship of listeners with the society at large. As preachers bear witness to trauma, listeners also become witnesses to these stories and experiences. The pulpit is also a space in which trauma can be triggered or ignored.

---

16. Long, *Witness of Preaching*, 47.

17. Long, *Witness of Preaching*, 49.

18. Long, *Witness of Preaching*, 50.

19. Florence, *Preaching as Testimony*, xxi.

20. Florence, *Preaching as Testimony*, xiii.

21. Morton, *Journey is Home*.

Thirdly, we are witnesses to the resurrection and the action of God in the world. The purpose of the church is to bear witness to what God is doing: "the Christian church came to be in witness to the memory of Jesus Christ."[22] Preachers are invited to continually testify to the potential for life in the midst of death. We are also called to testify to the death that remains in the midst of life.[23] As I discussed in the last chapter, in the face of traumatic experience we are faced with the "ambiguity, ambivalence of existing in an in-between space" between life and death.[24] We bear witness to promise of God that the future will be different from the present. Eschatologically, we witness to a future that does not grow directly out of the past—a future that is free from the grief and trauma of the present, that might provide some hope for trauma survivors.[25] Sometimes, and this is even more difficult, we bear witness to a God who does not seem to be acting. There are times when we must confront God in our sermons with weeping and a sense of incomprehension because we do not understand why things are as they are. We believe in a God who is open to challenge—a God who can take our critique and our lament.[26]

Testifying to the Reality of Trauma

Trauma is a kind of reality that the individual feels they cannot bear. In order for it to be alleviated, it must be witnessed. Shelley Rambo argues that the concept of witness "offers a way of thinking about a relationship to, and responsibility for, the past in its *ongoingness*."[27] This implies an ethical commitment on the part of the preacher to testify to the reality of trauma as it exists in the past and continues to permeate the present. The Holocaust redefined the concept of witness as the world came to terms with what it did not see and did not prevent. Bearing witness to the Holocaust transcended the ordinary and drew attention to death of an unimaginable magnitude. During a speech dedicating the United States Holocaust Memorial Museum in 1993, Elie Wiesel said, "For the dead and the living, we must bear

---

22. Keshgegian, *Redeeming Memories*, 200.

23. Rambo, *Spirit and Trauma*, 96.

24. See Cahalan and Mikoski, *Opening the Field*, 41.

25. Hess, *Sites of Violence*, 103.

26. Hess, *Sites of Violence*, 104.

27. Rambo, *Resurrecting Wounds*, 5.

witness."[28] The Holocaust reminds us that there are times when preachers have an ethical responsibility to bear witness to trauma. As Dietrich Bonhoeffer is purported to have said, "Silence in the face of evil is itself evil: God will not hold us guiltless. Not to speak is to speak. Not to act is to act."[29] In far too many situations in our world, good people have stayed silent when speech could have saved lives. It is necessary for preachers to acknowledge the trauma that permeates our culture and our pews in order to draw attention to the capacity for human sinfulness and the multiple ways we cause each other pain. Keshgegian believes that the church, as a body that remembers and witnesses, is a good place to talk about "forms of abuse, genocides, and the cultural histories of particular groups."[30] Narrating these kinds of events from the pulpit is a way of bearing witness to the pain and suffering of those who are near and far, dead and alive.

It is much easier to deny or cover up trauma than it is to bear witness to it. Judith Herman argues that an ordinary response to atrocities is to remove them from consciousness, as some things are too terrible to be named aloud: "this is the meaning of the word unspeakable. Atrocities, however, refuse to be buried."[31] At the center of psychological trauma is a conflict between wanting to deny the reality of traumatic events and "the will to proclaim them aloud."[32] There is a very real danger that even though trauma is present in our pews and our texts we will choose to stay silent. Trauma is taboo, whether it is caused by human beings or arises in the context of nature—it is painful, and it is in many ways "unspeakable." We may be reluctant to introduce painful realities in our sermons, preferring a happier and less fraught homiletic atmosphere.

To study psychological trauma is to come face to face both with human vulnerability in the natural world and with the capacity for evil in human nature. To study psychological trauma means bearing witness to horrible events. When the events are natural disasters or "acts of God," those who bear witness sympathize readily with the victim. But when the traumatic events are of human design, those who bear witness are caught in the conflict

28. United States Holocaust Memorial Museum, "Elie Wiesel."

29. Although this quote is attributed to Bonhoeffer, it is not found in his writings.

30. Keshgegian, *Redeeming Memories*, 226.

31. Herman, *Trauma and Recovery*, 1.

32. Herman, *Trauma and Recovery*, 1.

between victim and perpetrator. It is morally impossible to remain neutral in this conflict. The bystander is forced to take sides.[33]

The bystander is invited to share the burden of pain experienced by the victim. This is a heavy burden and an act of self-love and sacrifice on the part of the bystander. Preachers are often bystanders—while the trauma may not have happened to us directly, we see what happens to others, and we share their burden of pain. This is especially difficult when human beings are the cause of another's trauma, as in the case of sexual abuse, gun violence, and terrorism. In these cases, the preacher is forced to take sides—to stand with the victim over and against the perpetrator. At the same time, we also preach to perpetrators and must have the pastoral sensitivity to speak a word of hope and grace even to those who have permitted and pursued the violent wounding of others.

Witnesses will struggle to find the words to speak the truth, especially in light of the more horrific moments of human life. These events are found outside of everyday experience, often outside of language—there are no words that can adequately capture or describe them. Witnesses must activate a different kind of seeing and hearing—one in which comprehension is continually disappearing, one in which words fail continually and one must struggle to find meaning in the spaces between words. The "challenge of trauma is the challenge of witnessing to a phenomenon that exceeds the categories by which we make sense of the world."[34] As preachers, we must find words to express the incomprehensible, in the text, in our own lives, and in the lives of the communities we serve. To name trauma aloud requires a "unique set of capacities for those who seek to witness trauma.[35] We must be willing to listen, to bring to articulation those things that desire to stay hidden, to say things that are difficult if not impossible to bring to speech. Preaching can make space for the tenuous articulation of the unspeakable. The poet Audre Lorde tells us that "poetry is the way we give name to the nameless so that it can be thought."[36] Perhaps preaching is also an opportunity to give a name to the nameless, unspeakable reality of trauma.

In regard to trauma, the first step of witnessing as a preacher is naming events and situations as trauma. There is power in naming

33. Herman, *Trauma and Recovery*, 7.

34. Rambo, *Spirit and Trauma*, 31.

35. Rambo, *Resurrecting Wounds*, 5.

36. Rogers, *Unsayable*, 38.

experiences—giving language and vocabulary to identify and describe the very real emotions and experiences that shape our lives. In our sermons, we can begin to use the word "trauma" to refer to those situations in which people experience unbearable suffering related to negative events. Simply naming traumatic wounding in our culture and lives and texts can "begin to establish safety that can counter shame and grow into resiliency."[37] In relation to sexual assault, for example, Herman states that "the first task of consciousness-raising is simply calling rape by its true name."[38] We can name the suffering that accompanies a long illness as trauma. One of the most obvious ways we can name trauma is in relation to biblical texts. Rachel weeping for her children—that is trauma. Jesus's death on the cross and the confused response of his friends—that is trauma. While I am not advocating an overuse of the term, it is helpful to draw attention to the ways that trauma permeates Scripture and has impacted the history of God's people. Contemporary trauma survivors may resonate with the stories of trauma in Scripture.

Many trauma survivors identify shame as one of the immediate and continuing effects of trauma. It is a pervasive and common expression in response to many kinds of loss.[39] "Deep down many traumatized people are even more haunted by the shame they feel about what they themselves did or did not do under the circumstances. They despise themselves for how terrified, dependent, excited, or enraged they felt."[40] Survivors may feel shame based on how they behaved during the traumatic event or feel shame based on how they have behaved since the traumatic experience. Brené Brown defines *shame* as "the intensely painful feeling or experience of believing that we are flawed and therefore unworthy of love and belonging—something we've experienced, done, or failed to do makes us unworthy of connection."[41] Shame tends to be hidden, which results in a sense of marginalization and further shame by those who are experiencing it. Shame seeks silence; it "derives its power from being unspeakable."[42] One of the things that naming trauma does is bring experience to light that was previously hidden. Brown believes that shame cannot survive

37. Baldwin, *Trauma-Sensitive Theology*, 77.
38. Herman, *Trauma and Recovery*, 67.
39. See Kaufman, *Shame of Grief*,
40. Van der Kolk, *Body Keeps the Score*, 13.
41. Brown, "Shame v. Guilt."
42. Brown, *Daring Greatly*, 67.

being named out loud.[43] "If we can share our story with someone who responds with empathy and understanding, shame can't survive."[44] The very act of naming traumatic wounding may help to alleviate the shame experienced by some listeners. If shame is a fear of disconnection, as Brown believes based on her social science research, then naming shame as a response to trauma may aid listeners in feeling more connected and more worthy of love and belonging. Van der Kolk speaks of the necessity of naming shame out loud: "We may think we can control our grief, our terror, or our shame by remaining silent, but naming offers the possibility of a different kind of control."[45]

Witnessing to the Stories of Others

In sermons, we are invited not only to name trauma as a reality, but we are invited also to witness to the stories of trauma that exist in the pews and in the culture at large. Perhaps one of the most difficult tasks of preaching is to climb into the pulpit the Sunday after a global tragedy; yet few of us would consider preaching about anything except the thing that is on everyone's mind. This is the kind of preaching that is Kairos preaching—it addresses needs of the people in a specific time and place.[46] While it is vital that we preach about societal violence, pandemics, natural disasters, and terror events, it is also possible to include stories of trauma that affect individuals and communities on a smaller scale. While this must be done sensitively, we can address themes such as cancer, abuse, domestic violence, bullying, and other traumatic experiences that are likely familiar to at least some of our listeners.

Preachers offer a space to witness to the testimony of others.[47] Preaching is a conversation between God, the preacher, the people, and the contexts in which they live. For the most part, it is still the responsibility of one person to stand up and preach a sermon. Our sermons, then, are an interesting mixture of what we have experienced ourselves and what we have experienced within the community of faith. To some extent, we are continually speaking on behalf of others. In the face of trauma, we might

43. Brown, *Daring Greatly*, ch. 3.
44. Brown, *Daring Greatly*, 74.
45. Van der Kolk, *Body Keeps Score*, 232.
46. See Jacobsen and Kelly, *Kairos Preaching*.
47. Jones, *Trauma and Grace*, 32.

preach on behalf of those who cannot speak their truth in the public sphere, telling their stories, at least when we are given permission to do so. We have an opportunity to witness to what is often unwitnessed,[48] those hidden narratives of trauma that resist being named out loud. By telling the story, or testifying to the story, individuals may regain something of what they have lost. Agger and Jenson note "the universality of testimony as a ritual of healing. Testimony has both a private dimension, which is confessional and spiritual, and a public aspect, which is political and judicial. The use of the word testimony links both meanings, giving a new and larger dimension to the patient's individual experience."[49]

In the South African Truth and Reconciliation process, individuals were given opportunity to witness to their own experiences of the trauma of apartheid. Testimony, in that context, had transformative powers, as it enabled healing for many—those who chose to speak and those who exercised the option to refuse to speak. What if we were to make space within our sermons for the narratives of others? What if we invited others to the pulpit and gave them an opportunity to speak out loud, in their own voice, what they have experienced? In that sense, the preacher becomes decentered, making space for the narratives of others. Judith Herman names it as an act of liberation to create a space in which a victim can bear witness to her story.[50] Of course, the pulpit is the last place that many survivors of trauma would want to find themselves. Even in the quiet of the minister's study or in a coffee shop, it is an act of liberation to make space to listen to the stories of those who have suffered. When we are given permission to share those stories in our sermon, we may create such spaces of liberation for victims to hear their experiences narrated out loud and publicly in a manner which may lead to transformation.

In her searching of sermons preached by women at the margins of acceptable society, Anna Carter Florence discovers that preaching as testimony includes those who have preached and testified from the margins. Those who have suffered severe trauma and bear witness to what they have experienced are those on the margins of what we consider normative. Trauma is a marginalizing experience—it places people at the edge of culture and sometimes on the edge of their own lives insofar as they are decentered and disoriented. Florence also notes that preaching as testimony centralizes

48. Rambo, *Spirit and Trauma*, 11.

49. Herman, *Trauma and Recovery*, 181.

50. Herman, *Trauma and Recovery*, 247.

the role of experience in preaching. By witnessing to the stories told by others, the preacher takes seriously the experiences of others. If you will, such preaching makes space for a counter-testimony that challenges prevailing norms that would silence or ignore the testimonies of trauma. Trauma is given a voice all its own to make its own witness about the messiness of life and the potential for healing amid the messiness.

Testifying to Life: Ambiguity and Multiplicity

Preachers are witnesses to the resurrection and the power of God working in the world. Our witness is not always firsthand; it is wrought through the testimony of centuries of others—those who saw and wrote about it, those who have interpreted those writings, as well as through our own experiences of the living Christ in our midst. David Jacobsen suspects that "we will discover that the resurrection has unusual life-giving power precisely when the trauma or grief which we dare not mention is actually spoken and named, even while laying hold of the promise that resurrection represents."[51] In other words, by naming grief and trauma out loud, we are opening ourselves to unexpected power and to the movement of God.

Shelly Rambo, however, wonders about the possibility of witnessing theologically to trauma that does not go away. Suffering and trauma force us to revisit our traditional claims about death and life and how life and death are seen and interpreted and thus have implications for how we understand the term *witness*. She believes that if individuals and communities are to heal from trauma, we must witness to the complexity of life and death—the fact that trauma remains even in the face of newness. "Death is not an event that is concluded. Neither is life a victorious event that stands on the other side of death. Instead, trauma uncovers a middle to this narrative; it reveals a theological territory of remaining."[52] In this middle space between life and death, the witness is a hinge[53]—the witness is called to remain in this middle space, looking to the past to honor the traumatic event and looking to the future without negating the reality of the event. A witness, then, is one who sees and proclaims the suffering produced by what remains after a traumatic experience. Rambo calls this "witnessing from the middle." A person is able to view suffering that might otherwise "escape articulation,

---

51. Jacobsen, "Unfinished Task of Theology."
52. Rambo, *Spirit and Trauma*, 16.
53. Rambo, *Spirit and Trauma*, 40.

that emerge through cracks in the dominant logic."[54] While the witness is able to see this suffering and possibly articulate it, they are subject to "continual elisions' that make it impossible to see, hear, or touch clearly."[55] The witness cannot see everything—some truths are "suppressed, omitted, ignored, or passed over."[56] Such is the reality of trauma—it affects memory and sensation, and witnesses do not necessarily have straightforward access to an event. To witness from this middle space is to exist in a place of disorientation, where the strict binaries of life and death are undone. Time, place, and body become unstable when viewed through the lens of trauma, especially relating to Jesus's death and resurrection.

In this figurative, unstable site between life and death, the Spirit persists with the survivor.[57] The witness does not see the cross or resurrection, but instead stands in the space between the two: "The good news lies in the ability of Christian theology to witness between death and life, in its ability to forge a new discourse between the two."[58] In this sense, the good news is

> birthed from the middle . . . rather than one birthed from the resurrection event. The presence of the Spirit is more fragile and unrecognizable in the middle space. It is divine presence marked by absence. Forsakenness, abandonment, and alienation are truths of the cross that remain, extending beyond death to transform the landscape of life. The question for Christian theology is this: "is this remainder a threat to proclamations of resurrection, or is this remainder the seeds of witness upon which all resurrection claims must be grounded?[59]

The act of witnessing takes into account multiple stories and perspectives— and has a capacity to hold these stories simultaneously even if their edges don't fit smoothly.[60] The biblical text itself witnesses to multiple stories, voices, and theological perspectives. The church also witnesses to a variety of theologies and experiences and must find a way to hold these various realities in tension with each other.

54. Rambo, *Spirit and Trauma*, 40.
55. Rambo, *Spirit and Trauma*, 40.
56. Rambo, *Spirit and Trauma*, 40.
57. Rambo, *Spirit and Trauma*, 144.
58. Rambo, *Spirit and Trauma*, 7–8.
59. Rambo, *Spirit and Trauma*, 13–14.
60. Rambo, *Spirit and Trauma*, 151.

According to David S. Jacobsen, preaching participates in the unfinished task of theology. In line with the understanding of homiletical theology described in earlier chapters, Jacobsen views all theology as unfinished.[61] In dealing with troubling texts, he says, "The real problem with any theological interpretation of troubling texts is that the texts themselves are a product of historical realities that 'haunt' us still: grief, trauma, crisis, and other unresolved issues with which we are still wrestling—in short, an unfinished theology."[62] Texts witness to truths about God, but at the same time they wrestle with different experiences, including trauma, that lead to sometimes inconsistent, even conflicting truth claims about God, insofar as both the Christian tradition and the contemporary Christian contexts are haunted by trauma. Proclamation, that is, the witness of preaching "offers not finished health, but trusts God's unfinished healing at the sites of scars and pain. Such preaching might be more like a groping, stammering, ecclesial-sized, world-embracing provisional 'talking cure' by which we are sustained and anticipate signs of promised life until God's full purposes are revealed."[63] These are provisional truths, which we can hold in the presence of God and neighbor. To proclaim these provisional truths requires deep theological engagement within the sermon itself. Jacobsen envisions three theological movements that may make this engagement come to life within a sermon and may provide a way forward for preaching texts that relate to trauma in the text itself or trauma in our world today. I believe these movements can be used to respond not only to the text but also the contemporary context. In the first movement, Jacobsen draws on the spirit of the theology of the cross, suggesting that we call a thing what it actually is—naming some aspect of the text that must be claimed openly. This acknowledges that all is not right with this text or this condition. In the second movement, Jacobsen suggests that deeper reflection may take place about the theological or textual problem, in which the preacher admits how difficult it really is to make sense of what is going on. The question here is, What do we do with this text or problem? The answer may be that we do not know—we may not have an adequate response to the problem of the text or context. It is valuable to acknowledge the limits of our knowledge and understanding. In the third theological move, "the prior admission permits the preacher to say something different in connection to the gospel: 'We do not know what to

---

61. Jacobsen, "Unfinished Task of Theology," 408.
62. Jacobsen, "Unfinished Task of Theology," 409.
63. Jacobsen, "Unfinished Task of Theology," 411.

do with this text; but we do know this.'"[64] The preacher, at this point, bears witness to the gospel—says something that they believe to be true, despite the difficulty of the text or situation at hand. Gospel is named out loud, but the unfinished theology is honored.

Jacobsen's method is simple, yet vulnerable. It is an honest way of preaching, in which the preacher must be prepared to confess the limits of their ability and knowledge. The preacher confesses that there are parts of scripture, tradition, and the contemporary situation that we witness without having answers or explanations. We are not sure what we are seeing, and we are not sure how to respond. Engaging in this kind of theological discussion within the sermon, we are making space for the growth of the preacher and the listener.

Such a homiletical move neither replicates a troublesome text nor simply repudiates it. It neither reinscribes it nor erases it. It takes some aspect of the tradition seriously enough to take it up yet again, and to try anew—even if haltingly, in bits and pieces. It stays close enough to certain troublesome texts from contexts of grief, trauma, or crisis long enough to name gospel both with them and despite them.[65]

There are times, when faced with troubling texts or contemporary realities that we can only witness to what we have seen without being able to fully comprehend or theologize the situation. We attempt to name gospel into these situations, knowing that our answers are always partial and incomplete. We name trouble and grace, not always in equal measure, but to the best of our ability in that moment.

Walter Brueggemann also makes a claim for the multiplicity of voices and stories in the biblical text in his book *Theology of the Old Testament*. In accounting for the myriad views of God in the Scripture text, he views Israel as a plurality of interpretive voices that claim to testify on God's behalf. Theological claims in the Old Testament are spoken as testimony: "an assertion that awaits assent, is open to review, and must make its way amid counterassertions."[66] The testimonies of Israel were frequently in dispute with one another, especially regarding the exile accounts: "No one response was adequate and no one articulation of Yahweh in exile was sufficient."[67] Israel's core testimony was always subject to

---

64. Jacobsen, "Unfinished Task of Theology," 414.

65. Jacobsen, "Unfinished Task of Theology," 414.

66. Brueggemann, *Theology of the Old Testament*, xvi.

67. Brueggemann, *Theology of the Old Testament*, 710.

a counter-testimony, as the "good claims made for Yahweh as sustainer and transformer are offset and undermined by evidence to the contrary."[68] While it is the work of the witness to provide a cohesive narration of events, it is the work of the court to determine whether the witness is faithful and adequate.[69] Israel's bold claims about Yahweh were subject to cross-examination—"Israel's faith is a probing, questioning, insisting, disjunctive faith."[70] In that sense, the core testimony and counter-testimony are related to one another—this narrative/counter-narrative exchange is a way that faith is practiced. There is room in the narrative of faith for both testimony and counter-testimony. In this sense, there are "no absolute truths for us to own or access at will. There are only fleeting glimpses of the truth we see and confess in Jesus Christ, the truth that encounters us, in concrete human experiences, by the grace of God."[71] The context of preaching, then, is one of truths uttered and truths disputed.

I believe this concept of testimony/counter-testimony has implications for preaching and trauma and the manner in which we bear witness to traumatic wounding. I am proposing here two things. The first is that narratives of trauma provide a counter-testimony to narratives of grace. When we are confronted with wounds that do not go away, those wounds are a counter-testimony to any narrative that proclaims that resurrection is a triumphant and complete overcoming of death. It may indeed be difficult to see grace unfolding in the face of trauma and violence. I have already written about the ways that preachers may feel compelled to rush to the resurrection. The narratives of trauma resist any easy fix, even one as profound and grand and holy as resurrection. The narratives of trauma call into question the ability of life to transform death—death remains, wounds remain in the ongoingness of trauma.

Trauma narratives sometimes tell a truth that says life is not possible, healing is not possible. They draw attention to the limits of human capacity; they leave us wondering what healing might even look like. In some cases, they provide a counter-testimony to the gospel, claiming that life does not conquer death in any absolute way, that resurrection is not a once-and-for-all conquering of sin and evil. Trauma narratives, if they do make claims for faith, are much more precarious and tentative. They might acknowledge

68. Brueggemann, *Theology of the Old Testament*, 715.

69. Brueggemann, *Theology of the Old Testament*, 317.

70. Brueggemann, *Theology of the Old Testament*, 318.

71. Florence, *Preaching as Testimony*, 65.

that growth is possible, but rarely would they proclaim that new life sweeps away the old—one can never return to a pre-traumatized state. Preachers are invited to include these counter-testimonies in their sermons. They are a profound "but" against the story of salvation and redemption—Jesus came and suffered and died but . . . death is still here. We must account for the reality that death continues in our midst.

The second thing I am proposing is that preachers provide a counter-testimony to the narratives of trauma. Preachers engage with the faith community as one that proclaims the gospel—we preachers will not let go of the good news that we see. Our hope may stand in stark contrast to those who have lost hope or never had any in the first place. We proclaim anyway—that even in the midst of death, God is working toward life. I have already urged a less triumphalist view of resurrection that leaves room for the continuing wounds of Christ and community. We continue to proclaim resurrection, even if it has had a shadowy side that inhibits us from seeing grace in all its glory. "Testimony in public discourse narrates a story, a story that allows the transcendent, the possibility of the new, to break in and open us to change and transformation."[72] Along with Baldwin, Keshgegian notes that the witness of the church toward the victimized often fails to adequately consider their agency and resiliency. While trauma may not ever truly disappear, victims are capable of finding life that transforms the horror of the traumatic wounding. We not only testify to the traumatic wounding itself but also proclaim a counter-testimony—the capacity of life and recovery beyond trauma.

It is possible to hold these narratives of trauma and grace in tension. Testimony breaks all the rules: "it assumes that disjointedness and inconsistency are inherent to the life (and text) of faith, not to mention the character of the One we worship; it isn't remotely embarrassed to be caught holding core testimony and countertestimony in the same sermon."[73] In other words, life is messy and inconsistent, and it is acceptable for our sermons to reflect this reality. We can proclaim both trauma and grace in ways that honor human experience.

---

72. Chopp, "Theology and Poetics."

73. Florence, *Preaching as Testimony*, 75.

Truth and Reconciliation

One of the most difficult yet significant tasks for preachers today is to witness to societal wounds—fissures that run deep in the fabric of our nations. Oppression and injustice are sources of traumatic wounding that affect individuals, communities, and whole countries. It seems unwise to write a book about trauma without referencing the traumatic wounding of racial divide. In a chapter entitled "Surfacing Wounds: Christian Theology and Resurrecting Histories in the Age of Ferguson," Rambo argues that Jesus's appearance in the Upper Room testifies to wounds and memories that his disciples wanted to forget.[74] Their inability to recognize Jesus serves a purpose—they are unable to reconcile "this appearance within the framework of what they have known."[75] They are forced to see in a new way, to consider a new framework for viewing that world. Rambo relates this to our need to see differently when it comes to wounds of oppression and our need to testify to those wounds that we would rather not see. By "Ferguson," she is referring to the riots and unrest that took place in Ferguson, Missouri in August 2014, following the shooting of Michael Brown by police officer Darren Wilson. The shooting sparked a vigorous debate about the relationship between race and law enforcement. It was a terrible and symbolic event that brought to light the continuing discrimination and injustice against African Americans in a white-dominated culture. "The wounds of racism live under the surface of our collective skin."[76] Left untended, these wounds fester and are the cause of continuing trauma for whole populations in the United States and globally. This reality was particularly obvious in the summer of 2020, following the murder of George Floyd in Minneapolis. It is of course much more complex than a black/white divide. I have already alluded to the ways that racial and cultural injustice exist in Canada among white settlers and Indigenous peoples. These wounds are old wounds—they began centuries ago and yet still surface in highly distressing and destructive ways.

These wounds of injustice and oppression will manifest in different ways depending on the social location of the congregation, keeping in mind that many congregations will host a mix of social locations. For some, naming the traumatic wounding of racial oppression will involve

74. Rambo, *Resurrecting Wounds*, 71.

75. Rambo, *Resurrecting Wounds*, 81.

76. Rambo, *Resurrecting Wounds*, 71.

naming their own experience of such, especially for marginalized persons or culturally homogenous congregations that have a shared experience of such wounding. Other congregations will have to come to terms with their participation in oppression. Listeners may be victims, perpetrators, or bystanders. For all, the preacher serves as a witness to name out loud the presence of traumatic wounding due to racial divisiveness, whether they approach it from the perspective of perpetrator or victim. The preacher's role is to bear witness to the wounding, allowing its presence to disturb and unsettle the existing frameworks of understanding that exist within the congregation. Like the disciples confronted with the risen Christ's wounded body, the presence of traumatic wounding in the congregation forces us to see the world in a new way. Sometimes, we must bear witness to our own complicity and participation in acts of trauma. The danger, of course, is that we preachers will offer spiritual bandages that cover up the wounds. Rather than healing brought by tending the wounds, they fester underneath the surface of the skin. Christianity has certainly been guilty of both creating and covering wounds historically in its complicity with systematic oppression and colonialism. When resurrection is proclaimed as a magic cure-all for the ailments of history, we stand in danger of ignoring systematic oppressions. Rambo refers to this as a "Band-Aid narrative" that "spiritualizes, interiorizes, or privatizes the wounds. Wounds become symbols for sin or human limitation, but they are unable to speak about the wounds of race."[77] Naming, or witnessing to the wounds, "rips off the bandage" in a manner of speaking—bringing the wounds to the surface so they can be acknowledged, examined, and, perhaps, healed.

As I argued previously, beautiful words are not enough to atone for trauma. There must be a concrete, bodily implication for our preaching. In that sense, the preacher must offer a vision for how the listeners can continue the sermon beyond the sermon. The preacher witnesses to what God is doing in the world and invites listeners to find a way to align themselves with what God is accomplishing. The hope is that the act of witnessing becomes an act of reconciliation. Kaethe Weingarten writes that reconciliation can only proceed if people speak the truth in a context "that has been prepared by practice in listening carefully to each other, without defensiveness."[78] The goal of revealing such pain is to create a context in which people can forge new relationships. For truth to be

77. Rambo, *Resurrecting Wounds*, 74.

78. Weingarten, *Common Shock*, 178.

spoken, there must be a witness who hears without judging that which the victim is enabled to speak out loud. In this sense, witnessing is an act of remembering. "When we are witnessed, or when we witness ourselves, we are remembered. Parts of ourselves that have been scattered, shattered or forgotten are brought back together."[79] The body of Christ has been broken, and it must be remembered.

A Difficult Task

Preaching about trauma is a difficult task. I confess that there were times in the writing of this book that I did not want to continue. Researching and writing about trauma is somewhat traumatizing in itself. It became difficult to go back to the literature, to become aware of the stories of others that I did not want to know. I recall reading Elie Wiesel's book *Night* a few years ago. There is one story that was written in that book that was so horrific that I could not continue to read. I won't recount the story here, because it is truly too terrible to contemplate. It was, however, a moment of realization for me—there are some things which, once seen, cannot be unseen.

Preachers will benefit from a strong awareness of their own responses to trauma and their own personal triggers. As witnesses to the wider world, we may find ourselves just as traumatized by public events as those to whom we preach. It is painful for preachers to witness such things in our world and in the lives of the parishioners we care so much about. One of the reasons such bearing witness is so difficult is that it makes the events real in the lives of both those who experienced them firsthand and those who hear about them afterwards. Once we have seen we cannot unsee. Preachers may also be traumatized by coming to know about the traumatic events that shape the lives of others, insofar as "the violence that undoes you becomes, quite literally, my own."[80] As witnesses, we may feel shame, loss, or disorientation, especially as we are forced to confront the middle space between life and death. Healing, however, cannot happen unless witnessing occurs. If witnessing is a first step toward recovery, as Herman insists, then it is an act of sacrifice and self-giving to bear witness to the pain of others and name it out loud.

All these things that I have written about the preacher also apply to listeners. Listeners may find it difficult to hear trauma spoken out

79. Weingarten, *Common Shock*, 196.
80. Jones, *Trauma and Grace*, 14.

loud—whether it is because they would prefer not to know or because it acts as a trigger for their own traumatic woundings. However, the body of Christ is invited to bear one another's burdens, and becoming a body that witnesses to trauma is an important aspect of this burden-bearing. It is important to respect the personal boundaries of listeners, warning them beforehand if there may be elements of the sermon that they might experience as triggers. Listeners should always have permission to leave the sanctuary without risk of judgment or censure.

Kaethe Weingarten has written about *compassionate witnessing*, which is the ability to create a common bond with those who are different from ourselves. Witnesses are in danger of being overwhelmed, just as those who experienced the initial trauma and are suffering from it. Compassionate witnessing involves human connection and an awareness on the part of the witness about how they themselves are reacting and responding to the event. Weingarten also perceives that witnesses will benefit from a feeling of being empowered—effective and capable of responding to the traumatic experience they are witnessing.[81] While witnessing the pain of others is disturbing, it also bears a certain beauty—in that the speaker is benefitting from speaking truth out loud and we are able to coexist in that moment.[82] We will find ourselves amazed by the tenacity and ability of victims of trauma to survive, and thrive, in the midst of the worst that life can deal. Witnessing begins in listening but ends with the transformation of the world.[83]

"Christian witness will always hinge on the question, *Can we really say that, even though we have no proof beyond what we have seen and believed?*"[84] Here we return to the question that I was asking at the beginning of this book when I encountered difficulty writing a sermon about restoration. Can I really say that restoration is possible when it doesn't seem so? Can I really say that life will be different for those who have suffered trauma just because I myself have seen the risen Christ? Preaching as testimony is, according to Anna Carter Florence, an emancipatory and freeing act.[85] We are free to say what we have seen and what we believe about it, even when our experience may be different than others. Our witness to the risen Christ, whom we have (hopefully) seen in our own lives, may then become

81. Weingarten, *Common Shock*, ch. 5.

82. Weingarten, *Common Shock*, 231.

83. Keshgegian, *Redeeming Memories*, 236.

84. Florence, *Preaching as Testimony*, xviii.

85. Florence, *Preaching as Testimony*, xviii.

a guidepost for others who cannot see and have not seen. Our witness to grace may be a guidepost for others who cannot see and have not seen. When we proclaim and testify to our own encounters with a living God, we might just offer hope to those who are still waiting. This work of witnessing itself becomes redemptive when we are forced to go deep into the narratives and promises that sustain our own faith. We offer a tentative and precarious word that may indeed bring healing. While preaching must find a word to speak, in the end, is it not our words—no matter how beautiful—that will promote healing from trauma. It is the Word—God's acting in and through history in ways that we cannot always see or name.

4

Preaching In Between: Midwifing the Imagination

I took my young daughter to see the movie *Peter Rabbit*, expecting a warm and fuzzy movie appropriate for small children. I was surprised by the violence and trauma present in this film. The small rabbits are fighting for their lives against the evil Mr. McGregor, who enjoyed eating a rabbit pie made from their mother! They are orphaned, reduced to stealing food from the garden in order to survive. I began to think about the presence of trauma in children's stories. Most fairy-tale story lines encompass trauma—Snow White is poisoned by an apple; Elsa and Anna are orphaned and subject to a power that shapes their lives in negative ways; the little mermaid relates to an authoritarian father and gives up her voice (and her tail) in order to escape. Most of the heroines are orphans, some with evil stepmothers, all trying to escape some wicked person or experience. We are raised on the narratives of trauma. In these stories, however, the princess always finds a way out—she always finds her prince. So, in another way, we are shaped to believe that trauma can be escaped, that there is an easy way out, usually at the hands of a benign savior. As we have seen so far in this book, trauma in real life doesn't always have an easy way out. It lingers; the past shapes the present in sometimes terrifying ways. In every way, however, trauma has to do with imagination. Recovery from trauma involves imagining a new life that can integrate the old life. In the words of Judith Butler,

> Places are lost—destroyed, vacated, barred—but then there is some new place, and it is not the first, never can be the first. And so there is an impossibility housed at the site of this new place. What is new, newness itself, is founded upon the loss of original place, and so it is a newness that has within it a sense of belatedness, of

coming after, and of being thus fundamentally determined by a past that continues to inform it. And so this past is not actually past in the sense of "over," since it continues as an animating absence in the presence.[1]

A new place is found, but it continues to be informed by the past. This chapter wonders about the role of preaching in healing, resilience, and recovery from traumatic injury. Chapter 1 outlined some of the ways that trauma inhibits both language and imagination. This inhibition creates a challenge for the task of preaching, but preaching can also build the capacity of traumatized persons to bring their pain to expression and shape imagination—thereby increasing the agency and capacity to act. The goal of preaching in this instance is "to provide a space in which traumatized persons can survive and flourish."[2] This survival and flourishing can be addressed by perceiving the sermon as an act of midwifing imagination, a process of constructing communal identity and a process of embodying.

The Preacher as Midwife

Trauma can "override your powers of both action and imagination."[3] Thus, it decapacitates both imagination and agency, the ability to choose and follow an action. In fact, traumatic wounding has been called a "disease due essentially to a disordered imagination."[4] Trauma disorders our individual and collective imaginations, inhibiting our ability to tell stories that lead to flourishing. Loss can make us unable to imagine a future and to see ourselves as effective agents in the world. As Christians, one of our fundamental capacities is to be able to imagine grace—the grace of God acting in Jesus Christ and through the Holy Spirit. This grace is hard enough to grasp for those of us who are whole and untainted by personally traumatic events. How much more difficult for those whose lives have been altered by events that seemingly constitute the opposite of grace? "Violence has a traumatizing effect on one's capacity to imagine grace, particularly in relation to language."[5] Moreover, some, especially those who experienced developmental trauma that has plagued them since childhood, may not believe that

1. Eng et al., *Loss*, 468.

2. Hess, *Sites of Violence*, 90.

3. Jones, *Trauma and Grace*, 15.

4. Jones, *Trauma and Grace*, 30.

5. Jones, *Trauma and Grace*, 92.

they have experienced grace in the first place. How can one imagine grace when one has never experienced it? Even those who once knew the grace of God may have lost any sense of God's graciousness. Trauma fundamentally changes the way we see the world:

> The trauma has made the survivors' old way of understanding the world unworkable. They need to abandon it and find a new way of thinking about themselves, a new way of understanding the world around them. Those who view their lives and the trauma through a lens of religious faith will likely struggle with their understanding of their religion—their framework for understanding how the world works and how they should lead their lives.[6]

Familiar frameworks can be shattered and must be rebuilt, primarily through one's ability to imagine God and future. Imagination is crucial to quality of life. Bessel van der Kolk writes about the significance of imagination for human beings:

> Our imagination enables us to leave our routine everyday existence by fantasizing about travel, food, sex, falling in love, or having the last word—all the things that make life interesting. Imagination gives us the opportunity to envision new possibilities—it is an essential launchpad for making our hopes come true. It fires our creativity, relieves our boredom, alleviates our pain, enhances our pleasure, and enriches our most intimate relationships. When people are compulsively and constantly pulled back into the past, to the last time they felt intense involvement and deep emotions, they suffer from a failure of imagination, a loss of the mental flexibility. Without imagination there is no hope, no chance to envision a better future, no place to go, no goal to reach.[7]

The previous chapter discussed preacher as witness—one who sees and speaks. This section wonders how preaching can reanimate the imagination that has been paralyzed by trauma in order to lead to a retelling of one's life story. How can the preacher assist in this act of recapacitating imagination and agency? I propose that we can think of a preacher as a midwife of the imagination. Midwives have very specific tasks. They accompany the woman who is in labor—listening, calming, and preparing for the birth of the baby. They are skilled at interpreting signs of movement and readiness, as well as the despair that might accompany the pain

---

6. Rendon, *Upside*, §2033.

7. Van der Kolk, *Body Keeps Score*, 17.

of labor. They watch carefully for complications. They work hard, but they do not perform the work of labor—that is the sole job of the laboring woman. In the end, they troubleshoot and catch the child as it emerges—continuing to accompany the mother through the earliest hours of motherhood.

> [The midwife] has to be comfortable in the labor room; she is skilled and compassionate in the bringing forth of life. The midwife does not create the child; the child has already been formed. The babies she delivers are not her possession, but a gift that she hands over. The midwife listens attentively to the heartbeat of both the mother and the child . . . The new mother has the opportunity and responsibility to embrace and nurture her gift.[8]

Preachers perform many of the same tasks when it comes to birthing a new story, a new dream, a new possibility. We accompany our listeners as they wrestle and struggle with God's word and its relation to the events of their daily lives. We listen, we calm, we encourage. We work hard, but we do not perform the task of transformation—that is up to the listener in partnership with the Holy Spirit. One of the important aspects of healing from trauma is for the traumatized person to find a place in the narrative that allows for hope for the future. After all, it is in "places where despite terrible oppression, in situations that may seem completely hopeless, that impossible song is invented."[9] In the midst of trauma, it is possible for new songs to arise that permit the anticipation of life beyond death.

Shiphrah and Puah were midwives in Egypt when a new king arose and exacted terribly oppressive policies on the Hebrews living in the land.[10] Theirs was a forced labor, and the Egyptians made their lives as bitter as possible. Despite the oppression, the Israelites continued to multiply, to the point that the Egyptians came to dread them and their prolific growth. The ruthless king had a terrible solution—ordering the Hebrew midwives to kill the baby boys as soon as they breathed their first breath. Keep in mind here that the midwives were part of the oppressed population. They had a horrific choice to make—to obey their calling to bring life or to obey the king's orders. Disobedience to the king would in all likelihood cost them their lives. They made their choice—they let the boys live. In doing so, they enacted an alternative consciousness that proclaimed a resounding "no" to

---

8. Rickard, "Preacher as Midwife," 13.

9. Mayra Rivera in Rambo, "Theologians Engaging Trauma," 230.

10. Exod 1:8—2:10 NRSV.

the traumatizing forces of Empire. It was an act of profound imagination to envision life in the midst of the deathly reality facing them. Their refusal to participate in the evil plan of the king took great courage. Isn't this what preachers do? We refuse to obey the powers of death that are caused by traumatic wounding, pulling instead toward a word of life in the midst of death. We envision an alternative to the present reality, choosing to imagine that a future is possible that transcends and transforms the present. Our traumatized listeners may struggle to imagine such a future, but we as preachers refuse to allow death to define or constitute the future even as we continue to acknowledge the wounds.

After the events in Ferguson, Missouri, the Rev. Dr. Eric Smith preached a sermon about the midwives in Egypt:

> [The midwives] had a choice between two alternatives. Smother the future on the birthing stool, or take to the streets in protest. Shiphrah and Puah did the latter. They took to the streets. Because they feared God more than Pharaoh, they took to the streets in protest. But that was thousands of years ago. We are alive today, in a very different world. But we have some similar problems. And our choices are a lot like Shiphrah and Puah's choices. Will we be tools of oppression? Or will we be midwives to what's being born next? Will we be obedient to the system? Will we play our role? Or will we be disobedient and work for a more just society, for a better system that does not sort us into different kinds of people with different kinds of opportunities and privileges? Will we be beholden to that old slaveholding soul? Or will we allow our national soul to be redeemed?[11]

We might ask similar questions about trauma. Will we be obedient to narratives of trauma that prevent a new song from being invented, a new future from being imagined? Will we work to address the realities of trauma or will we ignore them? While we will want to honor trauma narratives, we are still tasked with the responsibility of imagining a reality that goes beyond the trauma of the present.

Assisting people in imagining a future is not about determining an endpoint and leading listeners toward it—the end may not be clear to the listener or the preacher. It is, rather, about establishing a direction toward hope. Homiletical theology works in the same way to establish a directionality that leads toward resilience rather than despair without necessarily

---

11. Smith, "How to be a Midwife."

knowing what the end point may be.[12] As we have seen, we are not moving merely toward resurrection but toward a space in between—a "gappy, airy, disjunctive" space.[13] This is the space of imagination—a space between life and death, hope and fear.

Preachers are poets of the imagination. We employ the most beautiful and expressive language we can muster in order to paint pictures for listeners that can assist them in imagining a new world. Barbara Brown Taylor sees nurturing imagination as a central task of the church. By *imagination*, she does not mean fiction or fantasy, but a task in which the "human capacity to imagine—to form mental pictures of the self, the neighbour, the world, the future, to envision new realities—is both engaged and transformed."[14] Faith is more than intellect or emotion, it is a "full-bodied relationship in which mind and heart, spirit and flesh, are converted to a new way of experiencing and responding to the world."[15] In this way of seeing the world, we are converted to seeing as God sees and to live "as if God's reality was the only one that matters."[16] In writing about the power of a novelist to make us feel and experience things that we have not felt or experienced firsthand, Taylor notes that the imagination not only creates pictures in our minds but also makes them real, so that our imagination shapes our perception of what is in front of us. Imagination allows us to find the extraordinary hidden in the ordinary and prevents us from thinking that God is finished with us.

At our worst moments, both individually and corporately, we act as if that were so. We act as if creation had all been finished a long, long time ago and encased in glass, where we may look at it through the grime of centuries but may not touch. Nothing could be further from the truth. The Holy Spirit still moves over the face of the waters, God still breathes life into piles of dust, Jesus still shouts out from our tombs.[17]

Thomas Troeger writes, "An imaginative preacher can take a biblical text and create a sermon that sets to the Word of God singing and dancing in our hearts, empowering us to live the gospel more completely."[18] Troeger writes of three different kinds of imagination. The first, conventional

---

12. Arel and Rambo, *Post-Traumatic Public Theology*, 12.

13. Jones, *Trauma and Grace*, xiv.

14. Taylor, *Preaching Life*, 39.

15. Taylor, *Preaching Life*, 42.

16. Taylor, *Preaching Life*, 42.

17. Taylor, *Preaching Life*, 50.

18. Troeger, "Imagination/Creativity," 191.

imagination, uses the Scriptures, symbols, and practices that are familiar to the congregation to bring God's word to life—this is a space of holy meaning. The empathetic imagination stretches preacher and people to put themselves in the place of others—to step into another's shoes. This imagination bears the capacity to see beyond individuals concerns to those of others (known and unknown), as well as the planet itself. The visionary imagination is "deliberately attentive to the fresh and unexpected movement of the Spirit" so that the preacher can see God and the world in new ways.[19] The preacher gives fresh expression to the yearnings and longings of the human community, pointing to the power of God to act in previously unimaginable ways. All three types of imagination are significant for preaching that addresses trauma but perhaps especially the empathetic and visionary imagination. The capacity to see through the eyes of another and the capacity to bring to speech an idea or possibility for human life that transcends the present—these are gifts that preachers offer to those experiencing trauma.

Walter Brueggemann's classic book *The Prophetic Imagination* engages the prophets of Israel to seek resources for the contemporary church. Of the joining of *prophetic* and *imagination* he writes that it "leads inescapably in an artistic direction in which truth is told in a way and at an angle that assures it will not be readily coopted or domesticated by hegemonic interpretive power."[20] Thus, the prophetic imagination of the church is urged to speak in a way that undermines the powers that be. Certainly trauma, at least the evil and disruption that underlies it, can be thought of as a power. He writes, "We need to ask not whether it is realistic or practical or viable but whether it is imaginable."[21] Imagination comes before implementation—that is, we must be able to imagine something before we can preach toward change.

Brueggemann argues that the prophets were able to enact an alternative consciousness against the royal consciousness that was a reality for Israel. This royal consciousness produced a sense of numbness about death and undermined Israel's experience of suffering. The prophetic imagination cuts through this numbness to name suffering out loud and bring to public expression the fear and terror that is silenced by the royal consciousness and denial of death—there is no possibility of new beginning until death is acknowledged and faced. It is this articulation of suffering and grief that

---

19. Troeger, "Imagination/Creativity," 192.

20. Brueggemann, *Prophetic Imagination*, xiv.

21. Brueggemann, *Prophetic Imagination*, 39.

allows for newness to be enacted. There is no beginning without an ending. "It is the task of the prophetic imagination and ministry to bring people to engage the promise of newness that is at work in our history with God."[22] So too is the task of preaching amid trauma. We name the grief and suffering in order to make space for newness. As far as the church exists in a space of trauma, it is called "to engage in the crucial task of reordering the collective imagination of its people and to be wise and passionate in this task."[23] If indeed theology's task is to re-narrate to us what we have yet to imagine,[24] is there an extent to which preachers imagine for those who cannot? Our people may not be able to imagine grace, but perhaps we can imagine grace on their behalf. In response to trauma, we are tasked with re-imagining God and the life of the church in a manner that can respond to the worst crises of human life. The church needs to hold people up.

Flora Keshgegian perceives that the church is a community of memory—we remember in order to be transformed.[25] When we remember the suffering of others, the dangerous memory of trauma encounters the dangerous memory of God's action in Jesus Christ, which leads to a "memory" of a new future.[26] Dangerous memory "fights against complacency and timelessness, forgetfulness and distortion. It critiques the status quo, resists forgetting, recalls what has been lost, and enables hope."[27] Preaching, then, names the dangerous narrative memory of the church by remembering the suffering of multitudes but also witnesses to redemption: "the measure of our faith is how much our hope is grounded in remembering in such a way that the invitation of salvation for all remains open, even for those who seemingly have no hope."[28] According to Serene Jones,

> in classically Protestant terms, preaching is most centrally an activity aimed at expanding and deepening the congregation's imagination of grace such that we might be better equipped to live in and move through a world understood as a place of God's continued, unfolding grace. Here, grace is understood as the unmerited love of a God who desires that we flourish and who

22. Brueggemann, *Prophetic Imagination*, 60.

23. Jones, *Trauma and Grace*, 31.

24. Jones, *Trauma and Grace*, 21.

25. See Keshgegian, *Redeeming Memories*.

26. Organ, "Speaking the Grief."

27. Keshgegian, *Redeeming Memories*, 137.

28. Keshgegian, *Redeeming Memories*, 139.

gives us the power to seek such goodness. In this regard, preaching is an embodied, incarnational activity, a lively example of the "Word-made-flesh" in order that the glory of God's grace might be vitally experienced and known.[29]

Jones writes that there are three tasks related to this reordering of imagination. First, traumatized people need to be able to tell their stories. Secondly, someone must witness these stories. Third, both teller and witness begin the process of telling a new story that paves a different pathway through the brain.[30] This new story is a story of hope that is able to imagine a future. All of this is aimed at breaking the repetitive loop of the traumatic story and creating a new way forward.

Thinking about the flames of violence that threaten and harm, Serene Jones writes, "I ardently believe that the reality of grace is vastly richer and far more powerful than the force of those flames. It is so strong that even when our capacity to narrate the good-news story of grace is destroyed (as it often is in situations of violence), the reality to which it witnesses, the unending love of God, remains constant and steady and ever true."[31] Jones's words ring true for those situations in which violence is not the cause of trauma, but rather illness or other forms of loss.

Jones thinks about engaging the traumatized mind theologically as a means of healing imagination. In her thought, imagination is not a "complicated abstraction of experience," but refers "to the fact that as human beings we constantly engage the world through organizing stories or habits of mind, which structure our thoughts. Our imagination simply refers to the thought stories that we live with and through which we interpret the world surrounding us."[32]

Jones finds resources for retelling the future in the narratives of the Bible. In the story of the disciples meeting Jesus on the road to Emmaus,

> a barely suppressed hysteria registers in their voices; their leader has just been tortured and executed, and they are trying to make sense of it, trying to reorder their disordered thoughts. In the process, they are probably replaying the scene of the crucifixion again and again. As they recall—or perhaps they cannot remember—the

29. Jones, *Trauma and Grace*, 92.

30. Jones, *Trauma and Grace*, 32.

31. Jones, *Trauma and Grace*, §108.

32. Jones, *Trauma and Grace*, 20.

violent events that happened just days before, they seem to be stuck in a playback loop, having lost both their hope and their future.[33]

Immersed in the trauma of what they have seen, the disciples are unable to recognize Jesus when he comes near. In this story of violence, God is already present, already here. Jesus begins to speak and thus re-narrates the story the disciples are telling themselves. He pulls them into a larger story, that of salvation history. It is the simple ritual of taking, breaking, and blessing bread which eventually opens their eyes. The meal breaks the cycle of repetitive violence. Jones notes that after Jesus disappears again, the disciples return to a state of unknowing—struggling to be able to tell what they have seen. Such is trauma—a cycle of knowing and unknowing—belief and horror standing together.[34] "Whatever grace we see—and seek to proclaim—will and should be a grace haunted by the ghost of the violence it addresses."[35]

Jones finds another resource in Mark's unfinished ending. The gospel of Mark leaves us "peering into the gaping space of an ending that never comes."[36] Readers are left without the comfort of a confirmed resurrection, unsure where to turn next—there is no "happily ever after" here. The women go to the tomb to prepare Jesus's body for burial, and they encounter a young man in a white robe. They are so startled and scared by what they see that they run away in silence. "I suggest that their silence is the fractured speech of violence as it lives in their bodies and psyches, and I argue that their inability to speak parallels the experience of trauma survivors for whom speech, memory and agency have been undone by violence."[37] In this sense, Mark's ending may be less a narrative conclusion and more of a telos—a directionality that points toward the future and God's grace and mercy.[38]

While we might prefer more satisfying conclusions, Jones suggests that this ending more accurately reflects the kind of fractured speech that is characteristic of the traumatized. She writes that traumatic experiences "often leaves holes in the stories we tell about our lives. There are places in those stories where endings are abrupt and ragged, other places where stories are unfinished; in this way, violence creates open-ended narrative

33. Jones, *Trauma and Grace*, 38–39.
34. Jones, *Trauma and Grace*, 41.
35. Jones, *Trauma and Grace*, 41.
36. Jones, *Trauma and Grace*, 89.
37. Jones, *Trauma and Grace*, ch. 6.
38. Jones, *Trauma and Grace*, 86.

spaces filled with fear, silence, and uncertainty." A feature of memory for those who are traumatized is that the trauma keeps repeating itself, as if it can't find an ending to the story. "When this happens, one can get stuck in time, a place that trauma theorists refer to as an 'eternal present,' a place with no past and, even more tragically, no future, no direction toward which life unfolds. In this regard, violence cuts off thought midstream and leaves one stranded in midstory."[39]

Jones's words leave us wondering about the function of preaching to those who are stranded in midstory. To some extent, we offer an ending to the story that results in grace rather than pain and trauma. We are invited to complete the narrative, to imagine a hopeful ending for those who cannot. We cannot ignore the places where comprehension fails, where there is no easy answer, and yet "it is precisely at the edges of comprehension, the places where comprehension fails, that something else emerges and the possibility of something else arises."[40] The Christian imagination makes room to tell stories "about people who are agents in their own lives, with God-given grace to act, moving through concrete embodied history in time, coherently connected to their own pasts and the stories of others who came before them, related intimately to other people and to the good creation that sustains them, and looking forward in hope to a flourishing future."[41]

Another aspect of traumatized imagination is that a person often loses their sense of agency and no longer believes that they can positively affect the world around them or their personal outcomes through their own actions.[42] Preaching must consider the unending reality of trauma and learn to respond to those whose capacity to speak and act has been disabled. In the story of the women at the tomb "we find a script that calls, not for oratory and powerful rhetoric, but for silence. In that space of silence there is room for a deeper kind of speech: the language of gesture, of embodied communication, of the pouring out of soul in flesh that transcends the power of language to capture or define it."[43] The women at the tomb are unable to act in decisive and life-giving ways. They are stuck in a moment in which their agency has been disabled. Silence is the only response they can muster.

39. Jones, *Trauma and Grace*, 86.

40. Rambo, *Spirit and Trauma*, 10.

41. Jones, *Trauma and Grace*, 21.

42. Jones, *Trauma and Grace*, 92–93.

43. Jones, *Trauma and Grace*, 94.

In the story of the women at the tomb, Mark shows us what fear feels like, what it tastes like, what it looks like. The experience of fear and trauma leaves gaps in our stories; it does not permit us to tie up the story with a pretty bow. It is raw, and jagged. The grace of this interpretation is that it means the future is also wide open. It leaves room for the stories of others; it leaves room for the possibility of actions and of positive agency. And we know that ultimately there is redemption. "Trauma thus provokes the rethinking of endings, endings beyond which we cannot imagine but nonetheless survive."[44] Sometimes, our sermons will end with concrete applications and with theological interpretations that deliver solid hope. Sometimes, our sermons may end with more ambiguous theological claims that leave space for God to act amid the confusion. We need to think carefully about endings and how they will be perceived by traumatized persons. There are times when our sermons must end with powerful claims and times when they must end in anticipatory silence.

Preaching, Recovery, and Resiliency

What role does preaching have to play in the healing from trauma? While there are some people who will never recover from trauma, scholars presume that it is possible for many to find healing after traumatic wounding. That said, one can never return to the person they were before the wounding occurred. Trauma can never be erased, but for many it can be eased or transformed. Scholars agree on at least two aspects of recovery. First, healing involves the reconstitution of the traumatized self. Secondly, it is a process that occurs over time. Healing does not follow a prescribed pathway, but Judith Herman introduced three key phases of the recovery process. "Because the traumatic syndromes have basic features in common, the recovery process also follows a common pathway. The fundamental stages of recovery are establishing safety, reconstructing the trauma story, and restoring the connection between survivors and their community."[45]

Establishing safety requires that the traumatized person occupy a physically secure state and experience a state of psychological safety (overcome helplessness, fear, loss of control) and social safety.[46] The second phase is narrating the trauma. This can occur in verbal or nonverbal

---

44. Arel and Rambo, *Post-Traumatic Public Theology*, 8.

45. Herman, *Trauma and Recovery*, 3.

46. Hess, *Sites of Violence*, 67.

ways (such as art, movement, or play). In this phase, traumatized persons are encouraged to integrate trauma into their personal story to create a sense of wholeness. By placing the trauma in the context of their larger life story, it helps to create a timeline in which the trauma has a beginning and an end. This opens up the possibility of a future beyond trauma. "Survivors challenge us to reconnect fragments, to reconstruct history, to make meaning of their present symptoms in the light of past events."[47] During this phase, survivors identify and process their emotional responses to the traumatic event and attempt to establish control over intrusive memories. Once they have contextualized trauma in this broader narrative framework, survivors begin to move forward into the world. An important aspect of healing is the act of meaning-making, as survivors come to terms with what they have learned about the world, life, themselves, and others through the process of traumatic wounding and recovery. Some turn to faith. "In addition to the creation of a coherent linguistic narrative, symbolic representations of the traumatic event in forms such as poetry, music, art, bodily movement and religious ritual can also advance a process of constructing meaning related to the traumatic events."[48]

The Christian community can help at all of these stages. It can provide a safe community in which to share stories and hold one another up. Preachers can work to create a safe environment for trauma survivors where they can worship without triggers.[49] This may involve warning listeners about potentially triggering aspects of various worship elements and, as previously noted, ensuring that listeners know they have permission to leave worship without fear of censure.

The church is the keeper of a special set of narrative frameworks that relate specifically to life, death, and resurrection. "These narratives, when internalized through communal practices, can help form or reconstitute church members' identities in a way that transforms internalized, traumatic violence and integrates and element of nonviolence into their being."[50] These narratives can contribute to helping survivors of trauma create meaning out of what they have experienced. The church provides supportive relationships and inhabits a community that exists across time

47. Herman, *Trauma and Recovery*, 3.

48. Boase and Frechette, *Through the Lens of Trauma*, 6–7.

49. Sancken, "Words Fail Us," 124.

50. Hess, *Sites of Violence*, 89.

and space, which may help to combat a sense of isolation. Religious rituals provide structure and predictability.[51]

A point for creative imagination is to explore how and in what ways the journey of trauma exposure, response, processing, and resiliency can find space and honor within our ritual structures. Would this simply require an opening up of awareness to the trauma already voiced in our rituals surrounding crucifixion and resurrection, or those of creation, violation, and desire for restoration? Or do we need new rituals to midwife us through the process of trauma recovery?[52]

Preaching is just such a religious ritual, which occurs regularly and often employs a predictable set of practices. I have argued that the task of preaching must consider traumatic wounding as part of its context and act as a midwife of the imagination. Preaching also has a role to play in the task of integration. Trauma is a disorienting reality in which life as it is disintegrates. Reintegrating, reorienting, is a goal of the healing sciences that aim to address the complexities of trauma. Rambo writes, "the vision of integration is one of befriending the world again, of restoring trust and connections, and finding avenues by which that experience can be placed in the fuller arena of one's life. Thus, the post-traumatic is the challenging territory of this work of integration."[53]

Preaching is itself an act of profound integration. We bring together God's word, God's presence, and the experience of people in ancient and contemporary times. These are knit together into some kind of cohesive narrative, even if we contradict ourselves at certain points. Preaching is a meaning-making enterprise in which we try to make sense of ourselves and our world—and of God's action in the world. We don't always succeed at finding meaning, but we attempt to bring out a word from the Lord that can make sense of the way that trauma shatters meaning in regard to "religious claims about lived existence."[54]

Communal Identity

Preaching is communal practice. Individuals are brought together in conversation with the word of God, with other listeners, and with the

---

51. Hess, *Sites of Violence*, 80.

52. Baldwin, *Trauma-Sensitive Theology*, 71.

53. Arel and Rambo, *Post-Traumatic Public Theology*, 4.

54. Arel and Rambo, *Post-Traumatic Public Theology*, 4.

preacher. The sermon, while it emerges from the mouth of the preacher, is a collective creation insofar as it relies on the reception and interpretation of listeners. A good preacher will have paid attention to the community in the creation of the sermon, so from that perspective the sermon contains the stories and truths of that particular group in that place and time. The sermon is a significant place of connection for those who have experienced traumatic wounding.

Connection with others is an important step toward healing from traumatic injury. "Traumatic events, once again, shatter the sense of connection between individual and community, creating a crisis of faith."[55] Traumatic events cause damage to relationships, and others within the social world of the individual have the capacity to help heal or to damage further. "In the aftermath of traumatic life events, survivors are highly vulnerable. Their sense of self has been shattered. That sense can be rebuilt only as it was built initially, in connection with others."[56] To what extent can the church provide a genuine, caring community, and in what ways does preaching facilitate the creation of such a community? Deborah Organ argues that it is narrative, agency, and connection that will provide a path to healing for individuals and communities that have experienced trauma.[57]

Herman believes that a social context must affirm and protect the victim through relationships with friends, lovers, and family. For the larger society, "the social context is created by political movements that give voice to the disempowered."[58] Churches form part of the social contexts and political movements that hear, hold, support, empower, and work toward justice. Trauma survivors can be helped along the way in their search to find their hearts again: "Finding our heart requires a loving presence who helps the search, who is not afraid of the painfulness of the search, and who can mirror back our buried and broken heart, returning us to a healing memory of our earliest pain and need for love. This loving presence and healing memory carry the profoundest meanings of forgiveness and remembrance."[59] Preachers can "emphasize the communal and collective nature of these practices

---

55. Herman, *Trauma and Recovery*, 55. See also Lifton, "Concept of the Survivor."

56. Herman, *Trauma and Recovery*, 61.

57. Organ, "Speaking the Grief."

58. Herman, *Trauma and Recovery*, 9.

59. Brock, *Journeys by Heart*, 17.

that guard against the individualism and, often, isolationism of persons and communities who have experienced trauma."[60]

Cynthia Hess argues that identify reformation can happen through the construction of a communal identity.[61] Preaching both responds to and shapes communal identity. Sermons are organic; they grow out of the context of the particular place and people. At the same time, they create worlds, participating in the social construction of reality. Preaching participates in the "entire system of symbols, languages, beliefs, actions and attitudes within which persons live and learn to organize and makes sense of their world and their actions."[62] Jones argues that this is an act of the imagination—our view of the world is constructed within these communal systems. Listeners come together from all walks of life, bringing their own memories and imaginations. One task of the sermon is to respond to these identities but at the same time shape a communal identity that is defined by the narrative of God's action in the world. This kind of knitting honors difference and diversity yet points the congregation toward a common identity and action. As participants in this process of shaping a communal identity, trauma survivors are drawn into a narrative that is shaped by the participation of all. At the same time, their experience shapes the narrative of the community. Congregations can come to understand themselves as units in which there are a variety of experiences, including the traumatic. The communal narratives of the church define our collective identity. As such, we become a community that remembers trauma but is also defined by a larger story of hope that does not negate the trauma narratives but leaves room for them to coexist with hopeful narratives.

Trauma creates a new place for those that have experienced the traumatic event. In the words of Judith Butler,

> Loss becomes condition and necessity for a certain sense of community, where community does not overcome the loss, where community cannot overcome the loss without losing the very sense of itself as community. And if we say this second truth about the place where belonging is possible, then pathos is not negated, but it turns out to be oddly fecund, paradoxically productive.[63]

---

60. Rambo, *Post-Traumatic Public Theology*, 12.

61. See Hess, *Sites of Violence*.

62. Jones, *Feminist Theory*, 33.

63. Eng et al., *Loss*, 468.

Does this loss of trauma then become constitutive of community, insofar as Christian community is defined by the collective losses that it together mourns? This is certainly what Brueggemann was saying in *The Prophetic Imagination*. If the community tries to overcome this loss by any easy reference to resurrection as a definitively healing discourse, then the community loses itself. Instead, Christian community, and the context of preaching, is animated by the very loss it seeks to overcome. In mourning together, we become what we are.

Embodying the Word

What does preaching do when words fail? I began this book by wondering about the failure of beautiful words, inspired by a traumatized person who claimed that words are not enough to atone for trauma. I have described some of the ways that words can address and respond to trauma. It remains central to preaching that words matter, even in the lives of those who are traumatized. However, preaching is about action as much as it is about words.

Recovery from traumatic wounding should attend to all the parts of a person, of which spirituality is one dimension. Preaching, of course, is not just about words. Preaching is an incarnational activity in which we participate, actively, in the gospel process.[64] "Preaching reaches the listener at the realm that lies beneath language."[65] If we look at preaching holistically, it is an embodied practice. It involves not only the context of the sermon but also our full bodies—gestures, eye contact, voice modulation; the whole human person of the preacher interacts with the whole human person in front of them. Preaching is a performative act—it accomplishes something in time and space, in a particular community. But preaching should pay attention to the body as well as the mind and heart. The body is a unique site of knowledge. "Homiletics names the body as central to proclamation. Before a preacher opens the mouth, his or her appearance, posture and facial expressions" signal many things.[66] Amy McCullough writes about one preacher, "[she] preaches as a body, alive to her passion, her strength, the internal communication of brain to muscle and her limitations. Her materiality rightly names preaching as a risky moment demanding her entire self.

---

64. See Bartow, *God's Human Speech*.

65. Childers and Schmit, *Performance in Preaching*, 156.

66. McCullough, "Her Preaching Body."

This is the gift and the ever-continuing work of exploring embodied life."[67] Baldwin writes about the ways that "theater, and other venues of embodied, narrative centered, engaged participation, provide an established structure with clear boundaries for safe and acceptable behavior that make it secure enough for people to begin to explore a fuller range of emotional and somatic feeling."[68] Preaching functions in the same way.

Homiletician Charles Rice has written compellingly about the ways that our preaching finds its place within the liturgy and among the sacraments of the church.[69] The sermon is only one movement within the liturgy, "the enactment in a community of what it most deeply believes."[70] He argues for an intense connection between preaching and sacrament. In sacraments, we literally act out the church's faith and the story of God's salvation. We hear, see, and touch water, wine, and bread. As a community gathered at the font or the table, we bring to life God's promises—we participate in a way that is profound and full-bodied. Sacraments open pathways for the intrusion of the holy in ways that words alone might not. While the violent overtones of the sacrament may be problematic for trauma survivors, there is a sense within the sacraments in which time itself is ruptured as the memory of Christ's saving act becomes lodged in the present. The dangerous memory of Christ's death at the table transforms into the possibility of a new future forged by body and blood. The sacrament, far from ignoring the material, physical situation of the participant, honors and makes space for physical and psychological injury. The sacrament also leaves room for mystery. Writing about the sacramental imagination, Shawn McCain brings us back to the idea of midwife, this time in relation to the sacraments: "our participation in the sacraments also enlists us as midwives, assisting the birth of a fresh movement of God's work and presence in our lives and our neighborhood."[71] In the sacramental imagination, our story is joined to God's story; we taste and see what is good and what is possible. We are also joined to each other. In the sacraments, we come together as a body—honoring the body of each one gathered and its need to be washed and fed. In this role, the presider is a caring presence whose role is to nurture the bodies of those who come together to share in

67. McCullough, "Her Preaching Body."

68. Baldwin, *Trauma-Sensitive Theology*, 67.

69. See Rice, *Embodied Word*.

70. Rice, *Embodied Word*, 25.

71. McCain, "Sacramental Imagination."

the feast or the bath. When words are not enough to respond to traumatic injury, the power and mystery of the sacraments may speak to the grieving soul in a way that speech itself cannot.

Putting it into Practice

This chapter has explored the power of imagination for healing from traumatic injury. The following sermon recalls many of the images and experiences I have explored in this book, including my opening vignette. It refers to the Parkland shootings that took place in February 2018 at Marjorie Stoneman Douglas High School in Parkland, Florida, which killed seventeen people and injured many others. A public outcry followed, resulting in the organization of a one-day march against gun violence.[72] The sermon draws on Serene Jones's interpretation of Mark's unfinished ending. It was preached during Lent 2018 at Emmanuel College at the Toronto School of Theology.

Sermon: Dormant Hope

Last Autumn, I was asked to write a series of advent sermons for the Presbyterian Church in Canada website. The lectionary text I chose for Advent 3 was Isaiah's vision of restoration about ancient ruins being raised, former devastations being repaired. And I got stuck. My mind was frozen in images—Aleppo, Haiti, First Nations reserves . . . Where was the good news for the devastated among us today? What could I credibly say to the outcasts, the poor, the marginalized, those who live amid the rubble of trauma unable to even hope? I could only come up with two choices. The first was to plant hope firmly in a distant and unknown future—The ever-comfortable eschaton, when everything will be made new. The second was to look for shards of blessing in the present day—the good work of Peacekeepers, NGOs, the kindness of strangers. And yet neither of these seemed adequate to match the audacity of Isaiah's claim. Both of my options were cop-outs, in a way, because I could not, even in my mind's eye imagine a situation in which restoration was possible. As sometimes happens, the mere act of writing a sermon drove me to the edge of my theological capacity.

72. March for Our Lives, "Mission & Story."

In one of those coincidences that probably aren't coincidences, an article landed on my desk by Shelly Rambo—a theologian from Boston University. She writes about being in New Orleans over two years after Hurricane Katrina devastated the 9th ward.[73] She is standing in someone's backyard. "There is nothing there," she says, "except for the cement sidewalk pieces and remnants of a washed-out foundation." One of the residents tells her "Things are not back to normal." The storm is gone, but "after the storm" is always here.

Rambo's work is in the area of trauma. She describes how traumatic events persist long after the events, and continue to live on in the bodies and communities of those who have been affected.

It might be tempting for us to try to wash away the trauma with easy words of comfort and hope. But that might mean that we "proclaim good news before it is time."[74] The suffering that is caused by devastation should not be easily wiped away. For many in our world, life and death exist in close proximity. Life remains difficult. If you have experienced trauma or loss in your life, you know this is true. It is impossible to restore life as it once was.

One of the most relentless and tragic results of traumatic experience is that it can destroy one's ability to imagine—making it impossible for some to envision new life arising from the ashes. As Rambo witnessed the suffering of the residents of New Orleans, she observes "Amid talk about building and restoring, these particular streets of New Orleans still are not restored."[75] Even ten years later, restoration is still elusive.

In light of that experience of my stillborn advent sermon, I read the story of Easter morning differently. Mark did not preach good news before it was time—his story leaves a space for the storm that remains alive and fully present in the lives of those faithful and broken women who were the first to attend the grave. Mark's original ending is ragged, jagged, and the reader's urgent hope for resolution dissolves into silence. The good news is there—you and I can see it, because we know this story like the backs of our hands.

But could those women see it?

They who had watched their friend die in the cruellest way—amid the hopeless brutality of colonial power. Every promise broken. They

---

73. Rambo, "Spirit and Trauma."

74. Rambo, "Spirit and Trauma," 9.

75. Rambo, "Spirit and Trauma," 15.

could not see it yet—could not grasp the reality of resurrection. They were seized by terror and amazement—perhaps still hungover, if you will, by the events of the previous days. They were not ready for good news—it was beyond what they could comprehend when their hearts and minds were frozen in grief and shock.

In the space between death and resurrection, hope is dormant. It exists in every real way, just as the seed or the bulb exists in the ground. But there is no guarantee that it will rise up. The good news of resurrection intrudes on the one thing we know is true—that death is death.

Isn't it? For Mary and Mary and Salome, death was death. They arrived to complete the tasks of death, having waited until the Sabbath was over. A Sabbath—no doubt, that was not about rest or refreshment, but about endless wondering and wailing and wishing, and walking the halls with tears streaming down their faces. In the early morning gloom, the strange angelic occupant of the empty tomb with his pronouncement of unexpected life, could not shift their reality away from the certainty that death was death. Worse even than death—was the mysterious absence of the body they sought to care for. They heard the news that Jesus was waiting for them, and we hope, at least for their sake, that they will be able to absorb this news and reverse their grief and begin to celebrate. But they do not. They are afraid. They cannot see the light of dawn breaking. And they run. What else could they do?

I've had enough of winter, and of Lent, and am in a hurry to get to Easter. But first, comes Holy Saturday. In my desperate rush to get to the good news of Easter, I almost forgot that there is a space in between death and resurrection. A space in which trauma of what has just occurred is more real and present than the hope to which we are supposed to witness. This space matters.

It is the reality of human suffering, and we dare not skip it or subvert it in order to jump ahead to a happier ending. There is a long and loud silence before Easter can make any sense at all.

I was reminded of this as I observed the news coverage of the March for Our Lives this past weekend. Emma González is a student and survivor of the shootings at Parkland School in Florida. In recounting the events of that day, she said "For us, long, tearful, chaotic hours in the scorching afternoon sun were spent not knowing. No one understood the extent of what had happened."[76] On stage on Saturday, her speech dissolved into

76. Aratani, "Emma Gonzalez."

silence—she stood quietly as minutes passed. The long and loud silence—in the space between grief and hope.

Perhaps those of us who have seen resurrection are able to speak that hope on behalf of others whose imaginations have been paralyzed. Yet there is grace also in the space of waiting. Our own resources will not bring life out of the ruins, nor cause it to spring up. A too quick or too triumphant gospel will not leave enough space for us to mourn our dead. As theologian Serene Jones reminds us, grace is grace.[77] It comes. It comes whether or not we can proclaim it. Whether or not we can imagine it. After all, we don't know what resurrection will look like. And sometimes, even when we sense the quickening heartbeats of new life, we will be too afraid to name it, too afraid to believe what we are seeing. But even if we run away, even if the good news is unspeakable in the face of unspeakable trauma and pain, life comes. Grace comes.

Thank God it is not up to us to make it so. Please God may we recognize it when it comes.

And if we run away, like those sorrowful women at the tomb, may we look back over our shoulders and hear the voice calling us toward life.

77. Jones, *Trauma and Grace*, 74.

5

The Bible and Trauma: Giving Voice to the Unspeakable

On June 1, 2019, Nadia Bolz-Weber preached a funeral requiem sermon for her friend, the theologian and writer Rachel Held Evans. The text was John 20, in which Mary Magdalene comes to the tomb of Jesus while it is still dark. Mary does not find Jesus's body as expected. Weeping, she confronts the angels in the tomb, saying, "They have taken away my Lord, and I do not know where they have laid him." Bolz-Weber wonders why it was Mary who was chosen for this particular task in the holy story:

> I think Mary was chosen because she was a woman from whom demons had fled. I think Mary was chosen, because she knew what it was like for God to move; not when the lilies are already out in church and the lights are on—but while it is still dark. Because unlike when the men looked in and saw only laundry, when Mary Magdalene looked in the tomb, SHE saw angels.
>
> Mary Magdalene saw angels, because she was not unfamiliar with the darkness. She had the kind of night vision that only comes from seeing what God does while it's still dark.
>
> I do not know why this is God's economy. That it is while we are still in despair. That it is while we are still grieving, while we are still sinners, while we are sure that nothing good will ever come. That it is when we are faced with the nothingness of death—that we are closest to resurrection.
>
> That is while it is still dark that God does God's most wondrous work.[1]

---

1. Bolz-Weber, "While It Was Still Dark."

In the face of trauma, we read Scripture "while it is still dark." We come to the sacred texts seeking comfort, seeking good news, seeking explanations for life's most vexing questions. We may or may not find answers. What we do find are others who struggle with God's seeming absence, with the continuing presence of trauma, and with great mysteries that transcend our ability to see and know. We read Scripture in the dark, and sometimes rays of hope pierce the gloom. Sometimes, we weep. Sometimes, we lament. For those who have experienced trauma, the Scriptures can be a strong resource not only for potentially finding good news but also for finding accompaniment in dark journeys. This chapter looks briefly at trauma-informed scriptural hermeneutics before turning to the practice of Bibliodrama and exploring lament as a language for preaching. As a preacher in the Reformed tradition, I cannot underestimate the centrality of Scripture for preaching. Trauma theory offers an interesting and necessary frame of reference for reading and interpreting biblical texts. For example, James Yansen has written about the Book of Lamentations, using the critical lens of trauma theory. He writes,

> Extreme violence tends to shatter, or at least significantly disrupt, the lives, identity, social networks and worldviews of individual and collective survivors. Many survivors experience a break with the past, present and future. Often, this experience of rupture in life challenges survivors to find creative ways of re-integrating their lives as they seek to regain a measure of control over, and a sense of normalcy in, their lives post-trauma.[2]

The scriptures of lament may indeed be part of this creative means in which the biblical writers reintegrated their traumatic experiences. These scriptures can also be a creative means of reintegrating the lives of trauma survivors today.

In the last two chapters I discussed the role of witnessing in preaching about trauma as well as the role of imagination. Textual interpretation is in itself an act of bearing witness, insofar as the whole of Scripture bears witness to the experiences of human beings as they encountered the divine. Textual interpretation is also an act of imagination, as we bring our creative insights to bear on urging the texts to life in our current context.

As any seasoned pastor knows, the task of preaching consists of precisely this: of inviting people into the stories, which, if proclaimed with passion and wisdom, provide them with just such ordering frames of reference. This

2. Yansen, *Daughter Zion's Trauma*, 24.

task is even more essential in the case of pastoral care for people suffering from trauma. Helping people of faith find a tale of compassion and grace in the stories of God's good news, a story capable of giving manageable shape to their many griefs and angers—this is central to the pastor's more intimate role as counselor and guide to the broken and the searching.[3]

Trauma-Sensitive Hermeneutics

In recent decades, biblical scholarship has paid attention to the reality of trauma and its impact on textual interpretation, interacting with fields of sociology, psychology, literary and cultural studies, and refugee studies, for example. Scholars have recognized "the manifold aspects of trauma, which include not only the immediate effects of events or ongoing situations but also mechanisms that facilitate survival, recovery and resilience. Trauma hermeneutics is used to interpret texts in their historical contexts and as a means of exploring the appropriation of texts, in contexts both past and present."[4] Trauma theory in relation to literary texts seeks to identify ways that trauma is encoded in texts, ways that texts witness to trauma, and the "ways that texts may facilitate recovery and resilience."[5] To the extent that literature is a form of representation that narrates the lives of those it represents, it can be helpful for telling the "untellable" stories of trauma victims: "Texts witness to trauma through their encoding of the not yet fully known or fully assimilated memories that are present in the form of absences, gaps, and repetitions. Texts become representations of trauma as much through what is unspoken as what is spoken."[6] Thus, the texts open a space of imagination in which we are able to insert our own interpretations of the trauma that is present.

Trauma theory, when applied to sacred texts, provides a particular lens "through which to interpret sacred texts and for rethinking the claims and central beliefs arising from them."[7] There is not a single methodological approach to trauma as a hermeneutical lens—rather, it is a framework that allows trauma in the text and in our world to come to light. Biblical scholars pay attention to violence, oppression, exile, and the ways that

---

3. Jones, *Trauma and Grace*, 90.

4. Frechette and Boase, "Defining 'Trauma,'" 2.

5. Frechette and Boase, "Defining 'Trauma,'" 10.

6. Frechette and Boase, "Defining 'Trauma,'" 11.

7. Rambo, *Spirit and Trauma*, 30.

these affect the individual and community. They pay attention to the ways that individuals and communities are traumatized, as well as the mechanisms for survival and resiliency.

Jennifer Baldwin identifies a framework for trauma-sensitive hermeneutics that involves lenses of alterity, multiplicity, empathy, and accountability.[8] I want to take these lenses and expand them to talk more fully about biblical interpretation for preaching. These lenses are intended to help clarify and illuminate, while preserving a level of suspicion in textual interpretation.

The *hermeneutics of alterity* acknowledges that it is difference that allows us to be together in compassion. As far as we are separate from one another, we are thus able to see one another "as being deserving of honor and autonomy."[9] This recognition of otherness "sets the condition for our capacity to fully attend to the multiplicity within society and within our self, the cultivation of empathy, and bolstering of accountability."[10] When we encounter the other in our midst, we have a choice to welcome them or to exile them. When we have such a choice, we can exercise agency, we can determine the course of our own actions. As we have seen, this is an important realization for those suffering from traumatic wounding, whose sense of agency may have been shattered. From the perspective of the hermeneutics of alterity, the text itself is acknowledged as other. Its context is different from that of the reader.[11] As the preacher interprets Scripture, she or he approaches the text as something other, a collection of experiences that represent people from a very different time and place. The text is allowed to remain on its own terms. Texts reflect the violent or oppressive situations in which they were written—a historical context of trauma. For example, the entire biblical canon was written by, and about, colonized populations. If we do not pay attention to the colonial context, we are unable to understand the true struggle that gave rise to these texts. By attending to the colonial oppression and trauma in the texts, we are able to work toward a more just, decolonized interpretation.

The *hermeneutics of multiplicity* recognizes that each person is created in a unique way, out of a unique context. There is diversity around us and within us. This internal multiplicity relates to what Baldwin identified as a

8. Baldwin, *Trauma-Sensitive Theology*, 79.

9. Baldwin, *Trauma-Sensitive Theology*, 80.

10. Baldwin, *Trauma-Sensitive Theology*, 81.

11. Baldwin, *Trauma-Sensitive Theology*, 85.

core concept of a trauma-sensitive theology and allows us to acknowledge the multiple emotional and intellectual responses we can have to situations or stimuli, particularly traumatic events. It allows us to honor the multiple sites of creative theological construction within our own tradition and within other traditions. "Traumatic wounding occurs when we fail to see the multiplicity of practices and doctrines within religious traditions, racial groups, and/or nationalities."[12] Sacred texts contain multiple voices and theological perspectives. When viewed through a lens of multiplicity, preachers are able to honor the polyvocal nature of the biblical text, recognizing that many voices come together to state facts and experiences about the way the world is structured. Biblical texts contain both the stories of those who suffer and those who celebrate, and the canon as a whole gives witness to the different experiences and realities of God's people.

The *hermeneutics of empathy* "facilitates our capacity to recognize connection and care."[13] Empathy allows us to listen to the experience of the other without trying to fix the situation, as well as seeking to prevent further traumatic wounding.

> Empathy begins with a pause in order to receive information as communicated by another without superimposing our experience or interpretation on top of the one who is sharing. It seeks to understand with as much clarity as possible what the experience was like for the survivor and then to join alongside the survivor as a supportive partner rather than authority.[14]

This lens seeks to "cultivate empathy between persons in the narratives, the reader, and persons in our lives."[15] Without empathy, we are unable to draw parallels with biblical characters or learn from their experiences of blessing, curse, and wonder. "Empathetic connection with the persons in our texts can provide a buffer against the feelings of hopelessness, isolation, despair, fear and/or helplessness that can overwhelm in times of primary, secondary, or societal trauma."[16] When preachers approach biblical texts with a hermeneutic of empathy, we make connections between our own experience, that of our listeners, and the experience of the

---

12. Baldwin, *Trauma-Sensitive Theology*, 83.

13. Baldwin, *Trauma-Sensitive Theology*, 83.

14. Baldwin, *Trauma-Sensitive Theology*, 84.

15. Baldwin, *Trauma-Sensitive Theology*, 85.

16. Baldwin, *Trauma-Sensitive Theology*, 87.

biblical characters—honoring the difference between them, but allowing our shared humanity to aid us in the interpretation.

The fourth lens is the *hermeneutics of accountability*, which brings into focus "narratives of traumatic wounding and facilitate the naming of those narratives as trauma."[17] This hermeneutic allows us to acknowledge experiences of traumatic wounding within the text itself. When we see these experiences, we are able to name them out loud and also able to acknowledge the ways that healing, resiliency, and resistance occur within the texts.

It is important to note that despite the healing possibility of Scripture, texts themselves can be traumatizing. God is often portrayed as violent and abusive. "A growing body of interpretation suggests that in many cases representations of violence in the biblical text, including those attributed to divine agency, can be accurately understood as symbolic representations corresponding to actual violence experienced by survivors of trauma."[18] These texts many transfer violence done at the hands of human agents to the divine, as a way to make sense of that which is incomprehensible. Preachers will have to decide how to honor the voice of the text while maintaining a hopeful vision of a compassionate God.

Bibliodrama

Preaching in a traumatized world invites us to connect deeply with others. It has become more common in recent years for preachers to interact with their congregations prior to the sermon in a way that involves the congregation in the development of sermons, for example, through Bible study groups that study the lectionary together, or through feed-forward sermon groups. I propose that Bibliodrama may be a way for preachers to come together with their listeners in order to more fully understand the impact of trauma and perhaps even facilitate healing. Bibliodrama is a form of role-playing or improvisation that invites people to interact with Bible stories for the purposes of education, community building, and therapy.[19] "In Bibliodrama the director reads through the selected text, stopping at points of interest to invite participants to step into the role of a character, or even sometimes of an object, and give it voice. Deriving from the Jewish tradition of midrash, Bibliodrama explores the unspoken in the lives of

17. Baldwin, *Trauma-Sensitive Theology*, 84.

18. Boase and Frechette, *Bible as a Lens*, 17.

19. See Pitzele, *Scripture Windows*.

the characters, the 'back story' or 'subtext' in the written narrative, even the spaces between the words, to bring the Bible alive."[20] It is a means of acting out stories so that individuals choose to inhabit a role within the biblical story—that of a character or an object. Such a practice might both educate and inspire preachers as they listen and interact with listeners in a creative context that allows for emotional and psychological connections to the text. Leony Renk points to Bibliodrama as a liberative and playful practice that attends to the experiences of women and other participants. It helps to express what would otherwise simply remain inside—the movement of God and the movement of the text.[21] She notes that biblical language is full of sensuality and physicality, senses which are usually overlooked in traditional biblical exegesis.[22] When paying attention to these senses, internal attitudes can be changed and bodily awareness can be increased.[23] In Bibliodrama, "each text is critically examined through the experiences of the bibliodramatists, and a lively resymbolization can be achieved . . . the text can thus be retold."[24] Working with the body helps to acknowledge the differences between us and can be a lively interpretational method for those suffering from trauma. In the method used by Peter and Susan Pitzele, the creative process is allowed to make the text more complete.[25] It acknowledges that the biblical text reveals multiple truths that are made evident in the different experiences and perspectives of participants. Obviously, pastoral accompaniment of participants is important, as emotions and experiences may arise that are difficult for participants to process. Renk views Bibliodrama as a democratic process that allows non-theologians to deeply interpret the text according to their own experiences. It is easy to see how such a process would expand the preacher's view of the text to include those traumatic experiences that arise within the process itself. Preachers whose ministry involves a great deal of work with trauma and traumatized individuals might consider becoming trained in the methods of Bibliodrama.

20. "What is Bibliodrama?"
21. Renk, "Where Do You Come From?" 312.
22. Renk, "Where Do You Come From?" 313.
23. Renk, "Where Do You Come From?" 314.
24. Renk, "Where Do You Come From?" 314.
25. Renk, "Where Do You Come From?" 317.

Lament

Trauma disrupts our relationships to others—human and divine. It can have a very negative impact on one's conception of God as well as one's relationship to the community as a whole. Biblical texts, however, function to reconstruct the relationship to the divine, "especially in the wake of disaster."[26] Human beings have always tried to make sense of suffering, and in the biblical text that happens in relation to God and God's sovereignty. The biblical writers don't hesitate to take God to task for the disasters and pain that occur. Tiffany Thomas writes of four responsibilities of preaching in the face of tragedy: to weep with the people, to wail with the people, to witness prophetically God's will to the people, to wait with the people.[27] To weep and wail is to engage the language of lament.

Lament is a theological language—a passionate language of grieving that takes seriously human engagement with God. Homiletician Luke Powery claims that lament "is vital for homiletical studies because it provides a theological language that embraces God and human suffering *simultaneously*."[28] As I have repeatedly emphasized, in the face of trauma it is necessary to hold in tension the pain and grief of trauma with the action of God in the world. There are times when our tears are wiped away; there are times when they continue to fall, despite God's presence among us. Lament can serve as a useful hermeneutical lens for reading Scripture in light of trauma and is thus a significant resource for preaching. "The lament is the language of suffering; in it suffering is given the dignity of language: It will not stay silent!"[29] Lament will not stay silent, especially in situations where it appears that God has stayed silent. This is an unresolved question, the one that keeps us awake in our beds. Are there times when God does not act? How else can we account for the realities of war and human atrocity? The fact that traumatic events happen at all? Even in the text as witness to divine action, there are spaces of silence. Lament is a way of responding to the silence of God.

---

26. Renk, "Where Do You Come From?" 15.
27. Thomas, "Preaching in the Midst of Tragedy."
28. Powery, *Spirit Speech*, 134.
29. Westermann, "Role of the Lament."

At the same time, we are enabled to lament because "it is one's faith in God that enables the believer to give voice to despair, which paradoxically claims hope at the same time."[30] According to Walter Brueggemann,

> [the] public dimension of grief is deep underneath personal loss, and for the most part, not easily articulated among us. But grief will not be worked well or adequately until attention goes underneath the personal to the public and communal. My expectation is that pastors, liturgically and pastorally, most need to provide opportunity and script for lament and complaint and grief for a long time.[31]

Most of us are much more familiar with psalms of praise than psalms of lament. In an effort to uphold the celebratory nature of gospel, we might be inclined to avoid the seemingly negative and baffling voices of Scripture that announce grief, sorrow, and longing. Soong-Chan Rah claims,

> [T]he American church avoids lament. Consequently the underlying narrative of suffering that requires lament is lost in lieu of a triumphalistic, victorious narrative. We forget the necessity of lament over suffering and pain. Absence doesn't make the heart grow fonder. Absence makes the heart forget. The absence of lament in the liturgy of the American church results in the loss of memory.[32]

Rah's comments are especially relevant when one considers the presence of trauma. Lament makes space for us to remember suffering—our own suffering and the suffering of others. A church that does not lament is not being honest with itself or with God. As Rah writes, "Lament recognizes a shameful history."[33] It accounts for all the injustice and oppression that have led to the way things are. If we are not lamenting these things, we are ignoring them to our detriment and the detriment of those who suffer. The absence of lament creates a "theological dysfunction" in which we privilege celebration at the cost of genuine lament for the way things are.[34]

Walter Brueggemann argues that the lament psalms perform a necessary function in the liturgical life of the church. "What difference does it make to have faith that permits and requires this form of prayer? My

---

30. Hunsinger, *Bearing the Unbearable*, 37.

31. Brueggemann cited in Swinton, *Raging with Compassion*, 121.

32. Rah, "Absence of Lament."

33. Rah, "Absence of Lament."

34. Rah, *Prophetic Lament*.

answer is that it shifts the calculus and redresses the redistribution of power between the two parties, so that the petitionary party is taken seriously and the God who is addressed is newly engaged in the crisis in a way that puts God at risk."[35] In this sense, lament is a form of empowerment—the petitioners (human beings) are putting themselves in a position before the Almighty in which we might be heard and answered. The covenant between God and humanity can only be honored if both parties have a voice. When communities of faith fail to lament, they are not voicing their pain and concerns before the One who can redress evil and betrayal, and thus the covenant is not being honored. If only joy and celebration are uttered, the covenant relationship does not reflect the reality of the people. "Since such a celebrative, consenting silence does not square with reality, covenant minus lament is finally a practice of denial, cover-up, and pretense."[36] In order for the covenant relationship to function properly—that is, for God to be God and humanity to be humanity—it must encompass both praise and lament. God, as one in relationship, desires sincere, whole-hearted relationship, which must include lament.[37]

Another function of lament, according to Brueggemann, is to name injustice, the reality that things aren't right, that life is not as it was promised to be. "The utterance of this awareness is an exceedingly dangerous moment at the throne. It is as dangerous as Lech Walesa or Rosa Parks asserting with their bodies that the system has broken down and will not be honored any longer."[38] These complaints of injustice can be leveled at one's neighbor or addressed to God's very self. Either way, they point to the fact that the reality of public life—the way things are—is intolerable. God responds to cries of injustice in order to rectify the situation. "When the lament form is censured, justice questions cannot be asked and eventually become invisible and illegitimate."[39] This is a point of access to God that demands serious change, and if this lament does not occur, Israel has lost a serious possibility of rectifying the situation and is reduced to despair.[40] Brueggemann argues that the reclamation of the lament texts is crucial because it allows us to be fully functional members of covenant and allows

35. Brueggemann, "Costly Loss of Lament," 60.
36. Brueggemann, "Costly Loss of Lament," 60.
37. Brueggemann, "Costly Loss of Lament," 61.
38. Brueggemann, "Costly Loss of Lament," 62.
39. Brueggemann, "Costly Loss of Lament," 64.
40. Brueggemann, "Costly Loss of Lament," 64.

us to address questions of injustice before a God who listens. In the words of Sally Brown and Patrick Miller, "Perhaps it is only in learning both to express and to hear lament that we can become sensitized to the often bitter and tragic ironies of our situation as both perpetrators and victims of violence and suffering."[41]

Lament in Scripture

The Scriptures teach us how to lament and, as argued above, give us language and permission to approach God concerning trauma and pain. Lament can be an important facet of recovery from trauma. Biblical lament is based on an expression of faith in the covenant faithfulness of Yahweh. It provides a "vocabulary of need [and] a rhetoric of affliction" in which the one who is in need cries to God to be delivered.[42] Lament is found throughout Scripture, most notably in the book of Psalms and the book of Lamentations. Jesus himself spoke words of lament on the cross. Sometimes, the lament scriptures appeal to God to adjudicate against human agents; sometimes, they lament a sense of God's absence.

> Rouse yourself! Why do you sleep, O Lord?
>> Awake, do not cast us off forever!
> Why do you hide your face?
>> Why do you forget our affliction and oppression?
> For we sink down to the dust;
>> our bodies cling to the ground.
> Rise up, come to our help.
>> Redeem us for the sake of your steadfast love.[43]

"The mode of lament reflects the psalmist's experience of profound disorientation or dislocation in terms of both external enemies and ills, and internal loss and confusion."[44] The psalms employ at times the language of the unspeakable. They hold God accountable for human pain and trauma and often move from lament to praise, proving there are times when lament must precede doxology. Psalms of lament, according to Nancy J. Duff, "1) challenge

41. Brown and Miller, *Lament*, xix.

42. Mays, *Psalms*, 23.

43. Ps 44:23–26 NRSV.

44. Hilkert, *Naming Grace*, 117.

our inability to acknowledge the intense emotions that grief entails, 2) free us to make a bold expression of grief before God and in the presence of others and 3) allow us to rely on God and the community to carry forth hope on our behalf when we ourselves have no hope in us."[45]

To navigate life without hope may indeed be the situation of many survivors of trauma. When this is the case, preachers and the community may be the ones to hope on behalf of others who cannot. The psalms of lament give rise to both a language and an attitude of grief and sorrow that relies on God's potential to act to change the situation.[46]

Rebecca Poe Hays finds within Psalm 78 a mirroring of Herman's stages of recovery from trauma.[47] Herman noted these as recovery of safety, remembering and mourning the past, and re-establishing connection.[48] Psalms tend to follow a particular genre—for example, the psalms of lament or the psalms of praise. Poe Hays finds that Psalm 78 is a mixture of history and wisdom. She argues that this mixture has the function of allowing a safe space for a traumatized community to recover from trauma and "reorient themselves to their covenant relationship with God."[49] The psalm begins with a wisdom saying, followed by an instruction for the people to pass on the wisdom to subsequent generations. It then recounts scenes from Israel's history that "move from disaster to hope."[50] The psalmist clearly blames the traumatic abandonment of Israel as a result of the people's sins. Psalm 78 "has no reservation about blaming the victim."[51] The psalm ends with a reiteration of God's faithfulness and nurturing love (vv. 67–72). It seems that the psalm did not address the traumatic suffering of any one particular community but was associated with communal memory of events that preceded the lives of the listeners.[52] By beginning the psalm with wisdom, the psalmist establishes himself as a trusted figure who is willing to collaborate with the people.[53] According to Herman, this

---

45. Duff, "Recovering Lamentation," 5.

46. Not all psalms give rise to hope. Psalm 88, for example, does not lead to hope, but ends in despair.

47. Hays, "Trauma, Remembrance, and Healing," 185.

48. Herman, *Trauma and Recovery.*

49. Hays, "Trauma, Remembrance and Healing," 185.

50. Hays, "Trauma, Remembrance and Healing," 189.

51. Hays, "Trauma, Remembrance and Healing," 192.

52. Hays, "Trauma, Remembrance and Healing," 193.

53. Hays, "Trauma, Remembrance and Healing," 196–97.

establishment of trust is essential for the next stage, which is to remember and mourn.[54] The psalmist goes on to allow the people to reconnect with Yahweh through a retelling of their communal history—they remember and mourn together. Finally, the people are reminded that God is beside them in the task of creating a future.[55]

June Dickie has also related biblical lament to Herman's stages of recovery. In terms of establishing safety, the very act of lamenting to a powerful God creates a sense of the existence of a protector and the reality of divine power.[56] Many psalms, for example, express confidence that God will deal with the enemy or the oppressor. This naming of the perpetrator, and expectation that divine justice is possible, can be very liberating for the victim. In terms of telling the story, the second stage in Herman's recovery process,[57] the sufferer becomes an agent by reconstructing their experience of trauma. This is an act of moving from silence to speech, which becomes an "act of survival, an affirmation of one's humanity."[58] When trauma incapacitates speech, as it frequently does, the biblical language can serve as a verbal substitute that proves language for expressing profound suffering that resists naming.[59] For those who have lost their ability to construct a narrative of their own traumatic experience, biblical texts may provide words and narratives that resonate with the experience that the individual cannot name out loud.

Soong-Chan Rah, in his book *Prophetic Lament*, explores the book of Lamentations as a prophetic critique of gospel.[60] In a Western culture that privileges other biblical forms, such as celebration, the book of Lamentations offers another view from a people who have suffered a great loss—the loss of Jerusalem.

As the people of God recount their suffering and their painful history, they call out to God in the midst of their shame and ask many of the same questions we ask today: Where is our hope even in the midst of suffering and death? Can we see God in all circumstances of life? Does our understanding

---

54. Herman, *Trauma and Recovery*, 175.

55. Herman, *Trauma and Recovery*, 196; Hays, *Trauma, Rememberance and Healing*, 202.

56. Dickie, "Lament as a Contributor," 146.

57. Herman, *Trauma and Recovery*, 132.

58. O'Connor, *Lamentations*, 5.

59. Dickie, "Lament as a Contributor," 147; See also Poser, "No Words."

60. Rah, *Prophetic Lament*, 25.

of a historical reality impact our current reality? Does our response to God reflect our understanding of a shameful history and a painful story that must be acknowledged in the face of death?[61]

The book of Lamentations is the story of a people who have suffered trauma and wrestled with the same kinds of questions that most people ask in the aftermath of traumatic wounding. Rah makes the important point that our lament, as a church, should include a full range of voices.[62] This includes those who suffer, but also those whose lives have not been deeply affected by traumatic pain. Sometimes, we lament on behalf of or alongside others, whether or not we share their experience of trauma.

Preaching Lament

Deborah Hunsinger claims that lament is a prayer that occurs *in extremis,* and that lament is faith's alternative to despair.[63] Lament entails a belief that God is listening, that God will not punish us for faithlessness if we express our pain and grief in prayer or our communal gatherings. Preaching is a space for lament, especially in response to trauma.

While God's grace is to be found in human experience, Mary Catherine Hilkert reminds us that "every assembly also knows its own share of grief and death that has not yet come to new life."[64] Announcing good news can only occur "if preachers take seriously contemporary experiences of anguish, impasse, and the absence of God."[65] Such pain must find a venue for public expression. Amid naming grace, preachers must name "dis-grace"— the pain and ruptures of sin that characterize daily life and world events.[66] The sacramental imagination, argues Hilkert, must account in some way for the reality of evil.[67] But where is there room in the Christian liturgy for lament? Preaching is one of those spaces within the liturgy where there is space and opportunity for lament. "If liturgies and preaching are to draw Christian assemblies more deeply into the paschal mystery that constitutes their daily lives, the community needs ways of remembering and ritualizing

61. Hunsinger, *Bearing the Unbearable,* 37.

62. Rah, *Prophetic Lament,* 208.

63. Rah, *Prophetic Lament,* 83.

64. Hilkert, *Naming Grace,* 108.

65. Hilkert, *Naming Grace,* 109.

66. Hilkert, *Naming Grace,* 111.

67. Hilkert, *Naming Grace,* 119.

the scandal of the cross as well as of celebrating the hope of resurrection."[68] Lament provides a particular form of dissonance that aligns with lived experience. While it disrupts the mood of praise to include lament in preaching, and in the liturgy as a whole, it allows for a more transformative experience of worship. Hilkert writes that the first step toward overcoming suffering is finding language that can help listeners to exit the "prison of silence."[69] As preachers speak on behalf of the community, they are called to name the complaints of the community against God. In the face of the very worst kinds of evil and suffering, sometimes preachers can only stand in solidarity and silence. To lament, perhaps counterintuitively, is to express profound faith and confidence that God will act, that God will not remain silent.[70] There is a strong connection between lament and hope.

Sally Brown argues that "faith truly grounded in the biblical tradition does not dodge suffering and evil by invoking a rhetoric of shallow triumphalism calculated to anaesthetize pain, drown doubt, and rationalize injustice."[71] We cannot testify in the pulpit to the good news of Easter without using the language of lament, insofar as Easter is always rooted and grounded in the cross.[72] Brown believes that lament can shape a sermon in at least four ways. The choice of form will depend on context and timing.[73] The first is a hermeneutical map for suffering that takes seriously our relationship with God and with one another. Scriptures of lament sound strange to our ears, and preachers might be tempted to avoid them altogether. However, the language of lament may actually resound within the ears of those who suffer. These sermons will likely begin by acknowledging both the divine presence and the situation of trauma or discord. "Naming suffering in concrete and unflinching terms is crucial."[74] The difficulty arises for preachers when the psalms of lament move on to call for the destruction on enemies. However, according to Brown, by naming this dark side of human reality, we "lay the full destructive potential of our suffering before God."[75] To name the enemy is not necessarily to point the

68. Hilkert, *Naming Grace*, 119.

69. Hilkert, *Naming Grace*, 119.

70. Hilkert, *Naming Grace*, 124.

71. Brown and Miller, *Lament*, 27–28.

72. Brown and Miller, *Lament*, 28.

73. Brown and Miller, *Lament*, 33.

74. Brown and Miller, *Lament*, 30.

75. Brown and Miller, *Lament*, 30.

finger at a community or a person but to acknowledge the myriad causes of our distress, including illness, natural disaster, and social systems that enslave or disempower. Even more difficult for preachers may be those texts that point the finger directly at God for human suffering. Such is our faith in a God that listens and allows us to challenge God's omnipotence and willingness to act. Fundamentally, writes Brown, lament is trust that God will make things right.[76] In a Christian sermon, our hope is in Jesus Christ and God's unique salvation in Christ.

The second sermonic form, which Brown labels *pastoral lament*, focuses on cries of anguish and pleas for a correction of the situation that has given rise to loss and disorientation. These sermons will connect the disorientation and outrage of the congregation with the experience of the writer of the psalm or other lament text, "giving grief a voice."[77] "Like sufferers of old, we trust our broken, angry hearts to the God who will not abandon us or the world."[78]

The third sermonic form is a critical-prophetical sermon that stresses the biblical modes of protest, resistance, and self-examination. These sermons will link the psalmist's cry of injustice with the injustices experienced by us and within our cultures. These sermons will protest the injustices before God and call for self-critical examination—asking about the ways we contribute to the injustices experienced in our world.

The fourth sermonic form is a theological-interrogatory sermon which will focus on God's action or inaction, examining the divine nature for response to tragic situations.[79] These sermons will ask difficult questions about God's nature and presence, interrogating the divine about why such tragedies occur and what exactly God intends to do about it. In Brown's words, biblical lament is "faith's outcry to God in the grip of trouble . . . a rhetoric that wails and rages, protests and interrogates, and finally whispers its hope."[80]

Luke Powery views lament as a "homiletical tongue of the Spirit."[81] His work looks at the language of lament and celebration in African American preaching, although he believes that searching for such work

76. Brown and Miller, *Lament*, 31.

77. Brown and Miller, *Lament*, 34.

78. Brown and Miller, *Lament*, 34.

79. Brown and Miller, *Lament*, 29.

80. Brown and Miller, *Lament*, 35.

81. Powery, *Spirit Speech*, 133.

of the Spirit is necessary in all ecclesial communities. Lament is a work of the Holy Spirit, and if preaching is to be truthful, it must lament.[82] Powery argues that in preaching, we cannot get to the height of celebration until we have plummeted to the depths of lament.[83] In other words, we cannot get to resurrection until we have acknowledged and grieved the death that precedes it. Powery names six "marks" of lament in preaching. First, lament in preaching names the way things are—we name the trauma, the pain, the concrete realities that shape our lives.[84] We name the unfairness, the unjust, the ridiculous. These are individual and communal. Secondly, the mode of lament is imperative and direct.[85] This is clear language, aimed at a God that does not shy away from direct and forceful speech. Third, the mode of homiletic lament is self-inclusive.[86] Speech is in the first person—*I* or *we*—and the preacher is clearly implicated and involved in the lament itself. Fourth, in the midst of lament, we name our faith in Jesus Christ.[87] Fifth, the lament eventually moves toward praise of God.[88] Sixth, the preacher employs heightened rhetoric—by which Powery means such devices as repetition and amplification.[89]

Putting it into Practice

My own experience with lament was forged and capacitated by the death of my son. As a pastor, I found public grieving difficult because I had stood in the pulpit so many times and preached the consolations of resurrection. My fear was that if I grieved fully and completely, I would unintentionally testify to something other than the faith I had publicly proclaimed. There is a sense, perhaps, in our rush to resurrection that we fail to witness faithfully to the pain that threatens to undo promise. As Andre Resner writes, "There is witness in wailing, loud lamentation, and refused consolation."[90]

---

82. Powery, *Spirit Speech*, 33.

83. Powery, *Spirit Speech*, 119.

84. Powery, *Spirit Speech*, 119.

85. Powery, *Spirit Speech*, 120.

86. Powery, *Spirit Speech*, 120.

87. Powery, *Spirit Speech*, 121.

88. Powery, *Spirit Speech*, 121.

89. Powery, *Spirit Speech*, 122.

90. Resner, *Living In-Between*, 17.

Rachel's lament appears in Scripture against the backdrop of the slaughter of innocent children by King Herod:

> When Herod saw that he had been tricked by the wise men, he was infuriated, and he sent and killed all the children in and around Bethlehem who were two years old or under, according to the time that he had learned from the wise men. Then was fulfilled what had been spoken through the prophet Jeremiah:
>
> > "A voice was heard in Ramah,
> > wailing and loud lamentation,
> > Rachel weeping for her children;
> > she refused to be consoled, because they are no more."[91]

Resner notes that most preachers skip this text when it appears in the lectionary in Year A, right after Christmas.[92] It simply does not fit with our festivity—it is tragic and horrible, and appears unpreachable. Here, however, we see the world as it is—a witness to a world that suffers unimaginable trauma. "Before the gospel can be the best news that we have ever heard, it is the worst news that ever was."[93] The deaths of innocent children rank right up there with the worst news that ever was. Who among us would ask a grieving mother to stop wailing in the face of the death of an infant? However, we do ask people to stop wailing, to move on from lamenting their great losses and pain. "The contemporary church commits a crime—indeed, it opts out of its true identity—I believe, when it tells Rachel that she's wept enough, that she needs to 'buck up and get back to praising: after all, Jesus has been raised so we can put away our tears.'"[94] When we preach in such a manner that it invites people to "put away their tears" in order to celebrate resurrection, we are dishonoring their pain and asking them to do something that the gospel does not actually ask us to do. Those of us who dwell in between the first and second coming of Christ are invited to weep and wail because the hope of resurrection remains, at least somewhat, unrealized on this side of history. In the face of trauma, tears may not dry up at all—and we have a responsibility to our listeners to honor their pain by proclaiming that gospel includes tears. Pain and promise belong together—such is the reality of human life in all

91. Matt 2:16–18 NRSV.

92. Resner, *Living In-Between*, 19.

93. Resner, *Living In-Between*, 19.

94. Resner, *Living In-Between*, 17.

times and places. The following sermon was preached on the First Sunday after Christmas, Year A, and is based on Matt 2:1–23, the massacre of the innocents. It is a sermon that tries to take seriously the necessity of lament even within the joyous Christmas season.

Sermon: Rachel's Lament

We have just celebrated the birth of the Christ child, we are still in the twelve days of Christmas, still gazing in awe at the baby in the manger, still feasting, still lost in wonder, love, and praise.

And yet, the Scriptures will not allow us to stay at the manger. Mary and Joseph and their newborn son could not stay there either—they are faced with a threat so deep and so dark that they must run for their lives.

The magi came to Jerusalem in search of the newborn king. They had seen a star rising, and being wise and learned, they knew that something was up—the atmosphere of the earth had changed, a tiny king had come to turn things upside down. King Herod learns of their search and interrogates them: When did this star rise? And what does it mean? Being canny as well as cruel, King Herod sends the magi to Bethlehem—saying "find the child—I want to worship him too." Of course, Herod doesn't want to do any such thing. The magi find their way to Mary and Joseph and Jesus, and they worship him, and leave their expensive gifts. They are smart—they know not to go back to Herod—and a dream confirms their suspicions. So they return home by another route—and they are safe.

Not so for Mary and Joseph and their little son. Herod is terrified—terrified that this newborn king will upstage him, that this newborn king will stage a rebellion, that this newborn king will threaten his riches and his power. It's hard for us to imagine how unstable and evil King Herod must have been to feel threatened by an infant. But it seems that was his nature. When he realized that the Magi were not coming back to tell him the location of the child, he was furious, and it seems that he perceived that his only recourse was to eliminate the threat—to systematically murder every boy child under the age of 2 in Bethlehem. Joseph has a dream.

An angel comes suddenly to warn him that he and his family must flee to Egypt immediately—in the dead of night with only the clothes on their backs. And so the holy family runs, escapes, and the little baby Jesus is safe.

But not so for the other children. There is a Christmas carol that we do not sing. A song that doesn't appear in our hymn books. A song that tells the devastating story of children who were killed because of Herod's despotic wrath. It is a heart-wrenching lullaby, a medieval carol that imagines the songs of the mothers of these children.

> *(may be sung or played)*
> Lully, lullay, thou little tiny child,
> Bye bye, lully, lullay.
> Thou little tiny child,
> Bye bye, lully, lullay.
>
> O sisters too, how may we do
> For to preserve this day
> This poor youngling for whom we sing,
> "Bye bye, lully, lullay?"
>
> Herod the king, in his raging,
> Chargèd he hath this day
> His men of might in his own sight
> All young children to slay.
>
> That woe is me, poor child, for thee
> And ever mourn and may
> For thy parting neither say nor sing,
> "Bye bye, lully, lullay."[95]

This song, this story, come as terrible interruptions to our celebration of the season. Mothers wondering how they can preserve the lives of their little ones, promising to mourn forever, saying goodbye. And in the words of the prophet Jeremiah, a voice is heard in Ramah, and it is Rachel weeping for her children.

To weep, and to mourn—to lament. And Rachel, that matriarch of Israel, refuses to be comforted—these mothers refuse to be comforted because their children are no more. What can be more antithetical to the joy, peace, hope, and love of Christmas than a story in which we find dead children, a leader's wrath, and an escape in the darkness? Lament is at the heart of the Christmas story.

To lament is to weep, and wail, and confront God with pain and bitterness—to cry out to a God of compassion and justice—to be incessant in stating our confusion and our grief. This might seem like an unfaithful act—after all, we are taught to praise God, and weeping and wailing doesn't feel like praise. And yet, what can be more faithful than turning to the One,

---

95. "Coventry Carol."

Holy God of the universe to demand answers—to demand comfort and justice and peace? Lament is the prerogative of a faithful people. We cry to God because we are in relationship with God—

Because we believe that God is the only one who can address our concerns, the only one who can provide comfort and justice and peace.

And so those mothers lamented. They lamented the wicked and evil act of a king who controlled their lives. They lament the death of their children and they refuse to be comforted.

They lament their trauma and their grief and the unrelenting pain of a situation in which they are pawns in the game of a system that takes what they love most. They lamented.

Even in the midst of this Christmas season, we hear the weeping and wailing of mothers whose children have been taken. Lully, lullay, thou little tiny child.

We hear the weeping and wailing of fathers whose children have been killed by gun violence, or detained at the border of the United States and Mexico. Lully, lullay, thou little tiny child.

We hear the weeping and wailing of grandmothers whose own children lie dead from AIDS and must now raise their grandchildren without the support of the younger generation. Lully, lullay, thou little tiny child.

We hear the weeping and wailing of Indigenous families who are threatened by mental health woes, whose children are more vulnerable to suicide, whose health care is faltering, whose communities are limited by a lack of education and access to resources. Lully, lullay, thou little tiny child.

We hear the weeping and wailing and what else can we do but join the chorus and raise our voices in lament to a God who listens.

God does not take away our grief—it is necessary and important that we grieve.

For our own losses—grieving is way of healing. For the losses of others, grieving is a way to stay in solidarity. We grieve because the world is not as it should be or could be. Our grief matters.

And it matters that we lift our voices to the Lord and ask for our grief to be honoured—but something happens when we grieve before God—when we lament—

We find that our lament begins to transform the world. God acts in and through our lament—

To bring about justice, to alert us to those situations and systems that must be changed. The activist Angela Davis once said: "You have to act as if it were possible to radically transform the world. And you have to do it all the time."[96] When we lament we are claiming that God has the power to transform the world and we are refusing to stay silent until God acts.

When we lament, we are acting as if it were possible to radically transform the world.

We cannot bring back the children that were murdered. Not Rachel's children, not Bethlehem's children, not the children who die every day on this very continent, and around the world.

But we can lament that children die. We can lament that mothers and fathers suffer. We can cry out to God and say "enough is enough." And we can remember that God weeps with us.

God too laments the human evil and systematic oppression that mar the face of God's good creation.

We can remember that God has already begun the work of transformation. In Jesus Christ, we learned that it is possible for radical good to overcome radical evil. In Jesus Christ, we learned that Good Friday does not have the last word. In Jesus Christ, we learned that there is indeed life beyond death. There is life, just as we learned through this tiny baby that was born to begin the work of radical transformation that this world so desperately needs.

We learned all of those things in Jesus Christ. At the same time, we are invited to stay a while, and lament what is wrong with the world. Before we move to resurrection, we must grieve the pain and suffering that afflict the mothers and fathers and grandmothers and grandfathers. And mother earth itself. We are invited to raise up our voices with those who suffer, to remain in the sadness and bitterness, to remain in the trauma and the grief, knowing that transformation is possible but being unwilling to move too far too fast while the earth still hurts. It is, after all, because of the newborn babe in the manger that we can see clearly what is wrong. Jesus taught us to look at the world with new eyes, to look for poverty, and oppression, and social sinfulness, to stay with him in the garden and weep. So this Christmas season, let us pay attention. Let us mingle our songs of joy with lament—in the sure and certain hope that God hears our cries, that the grief of the world is broken open in God's hands, that radical transformation is possible.

96. From a lecture delivered at Southern Illinois University, Carbondale, February 13, 2014.

Bibliography

Agger, Inger, and Søren Buus Jensen. "Testimony as Ritual and Evidence in Psychotherapy for Political Refugees." *Journal of Traumatic Stress* 3 (1990) 115–30.

Allen, Troy D. "Katrina: Race, Class, and Poverty; Reflections and Analysis." *Journal of Black Studies* 37 (2007) 466–68.

American Psychiatric Association. *Diagnostic and Statistical Manual of Mental Disorders: DSM-V.* 5th ed. Arlington, VA: American Psychiatric Association, 2013.

———. "What Is Posttraumatic Stress Disorder?" https://www.psychiatry.org/patients-families/ptsd/what-is-ptsd.

Aratani, Lori. "Parkland Student Emma Gonzalez Demonstrates the Power of Silence." *The Washington Post*, March 24, 2018. https://www.washingtonpost.com/local/2018/live-updates/politics/march-for-our-lives/parkland-student-emma-gonzalez-demonstrates-the-power-of-silence/?arc404=true.

Arel, Stephanie N., and Shelly Rambo, eds. *Post-Traumatic Public Theology.* London: Palgrave Macmillan, 2016.

Baldwin, Jennifer. *Trauma-Sensitive Theology: Thinking Theologically in the Era of Trauma.* Eugene, OR: Cascade, 2018.

Bartow, Charles L. *God's Human Speech: A Practical Theology of Proclamation.* Grand Rapids: Eerdmans, 1997.

Beste, Jennifer Erin. *God and the Victim: Traumatic Intrusions on Grace and Freedom.* American Academy of Religion Academy Series. Oxford: Oxford University Press, 2007.

Bethune, Brian. "Inside Roméo Dallaire's Ongoing Battle with PTSD." *Maclean's*, October 21, 2016. https://www.macleans.ca/culture/books/inside-romeo-dallaires-brutally-revealing-new-memoir/.

Boase, Elizabeth, and Christopher G. Frechette, eds. *Bible Through the Lens of Trauma.* Semeia Studies 86. Atlanta: Society of Biblical Literature, 2016.

Bolz-Weber, Nadia. "While It Was Still Dark: A Requiem for Rachel Held Evans." *Red Letter Christians*, June 3, 2019. https://www.redletterchristians.org/while-it-was-still-dark-a-requiem-for-rachel-held-evans/.

Brasfield, Charles. "Residential School Syndrome." *British Columbia Medical Journal* 43 (2001) 78–81. https://www.bcmj.org/articles/residential-school-syndrome.

Brett, Mark G. *Political Trauma and Healing: Biblical Ethics for a Postcolonial World.* Grand Rapids: Eerdmans, 2016.

Brock, Rita Nakashima. *Journeys by Heart: A Christology of Erotic Power*. New York: Crossroad, 1988.

Brown, Brené. *Daring Greatly: How the Courage to Be Vulnerable Transforms the Way We Live, Love, Parent, and Lead*. New York: Gotham, 2012.

———. "Shame v. Guilt." *Brené Brown*, January 15, 2013. https://brenebrown.com/blog/2013/01/14/shame-v-guilt/.

Brown, Sally A., and Patrick D. Miller, eds. *Lament: Reclaiming Practices in Pulpit, Pew, and Public Square*. Louisville, KY: Westminster John Knox, 2005.

Brueggemann, Walter. "The Costly Loss of Lament." *Journal for the Study of the Old Testament* 11 (1986) 57–71.

———. *The Prophetic Imagination*. 2nd ed. Minneapolis: Fortress, 2001.

———. *Theology of the Old Testament: Testimony, Dispute, Advocacy*. Minneapolis: Fortress, 1997.

Bush, Michael D., ed. *This Incomplete One: Words Occasioned by the Death of a Young Person*. Grand Rapids: Eerdmans, 2006.

Cahalan, Kathleen A., and Gordon S. Mikoski, eds. *Opening the Field of Practical Theology: An Introduction*. Lanham, MA: Rowman & Littlefield, 2014.

Caruth, Cathy, ed. *Trauma: Explorations in Memory*. Baltimore: Johns Hopkins University Press, 1995.

Childers, Jana, and Clayton J. Schmit, eds. *Performance in Preaching: Bringing the Sermon to Life*. Engaging Worship. Grand Rapids: Baker Academic, 2008.

Chopp, Rebecca. "Reimagining Public Discourse." http://www.religion.uct.ac.za/sites/default/files/image_tool/images/113/Institutes/Religion_in_Public_Life_ME_1999/Concep_Papers/Rebecca_Chopp.pdf.

Coffin, William Sloane. "Alex's Death" In *This Incomplete One: Words Occasioned by the Death of a Young Person*, edited by Michael D. Bush, 55-60. Grand Rapids: Eerdmans, 2006.

Dickie, June F. "Lament as a Contributor to the Healing of Trauma: An Application of Poetry in the Form of Biblical Lament." *Pastoral Psychology* 68 (2019) 145–56.

Duff, Nancy J. "Recovering Lamentation as a Practice in the Church." In *Lament: Reclaiming Practices in Pulpit, Pew, and Public Square*, edited by Sally A. Brown and Patrick D. Miller, 3–14. Louisville, KY: Westminster John Knox, 2005.

Eng, David L., et al. *Loss: The Politics of Mourning*. Berkeley: University of California Press, 2003.

Farley, Edward. *Practicing Gospel: Unconventional Thoughts on the Church's Ministry*. Louisville, KY: Westminster John Knox, 2003.

Felman, Shoshana. "Education and Crisis, or the Vicissitudes of Teaching." In *Trauma: Explorations in Memory*, edited by Cathy Caruth, 13–60. Baltimore: Johns Hopkins University Press, 1995.

Felman, Shoshana, and Dori Laub. *Testimony: Crises of Witnessing in Literature, Psychoanalysis, and History*. New York: Routledge, 1991.

Florence, Anna Carter. *Preaching as Testimony*. Louisville, KY: Westminster John Knox, 2007.

Frechette, Christopher G., and Elizabeth Boase. "Defining 'Trauma' as a Useful Lens for Biblical Interpretation." In *Bible through the Lens of Trauma*, edited by Elizabeth Boase and Christopher G. Frechette, 1–23. Semeia Studies 86. Atlanta: Society of Biblical Literature, 2016.

Fulkerson, Mary McClintock. *Places of Redemption: Theology for a Worldly Church.* Oxford: Oxford University Press, 2007.

Hall, Douglas John. *The Cross in Our Context: Jesus and the Suffering World.* Minneapolis: Fortress, 2003.

Hays, Rebecca Poe. "Trauma, Remembrance, and Healing: The Meeting of Wisdom and History in Psalm 78." *Journal for the Study of the Old Testament* 41 (2016) 183–204.

Herman, Judith Lewis. *Trauma and Recovery: The Aftermath of Violence—from Domestic Abuse to Political Terror.* New York: Basic, 2015.

Hess, Cynthia. *Sites of Violence, Sites of Grace: Christian Nonviolence and the Traumatized Self.* Lanham, MD: Lexington, 2009.

Hilkert, Mary Catherine. *Naming Grace: Preaching and the Sacramental Imagination.* New York: Continuum, 1997.

Hunsinger, Deborah van Deusen. *Bearing the Unbearable: Trauma, Gospel, and Pastoral Care.* Grand Rapids: Eerdmans, 2015.

Jacobsen, David Schnasa. "Gospel as Transfiguring Promise: The Unfinished Task of Homiletical Theology in a Context of Disestablishment, Empire, and White Supremacy." In *Theologies of the Gospel in Context: The Crux of Homiletical Theology.* edited by David S. Jacobsen, 138–55. Eugene, OR: Cascade, 2017.

———. "Homiletical Theology." *Boston University School of Theology*, Homiletical Theology Project. http://www.bu.edu/homiletical-theology-project/homiletical-theology/.

———. "Preaching as the Unfinished Task of Theology: Grief, Trauma, and Early Christian Texts in Homiletical Interpretation." *Theology Today* 70 (2014) 407–16.

———, ed. *Homiletical Theology: Preaching as Doing Theology.* Vol. 1 of *Promise of Homiletical Theology.* Eugene, OR: Cascade, 2015.

———, ed. *Theologies of the Gospel in Context: The Crux of Homiletical Theology.* Vol. 3 of *The Promise of Homiletical Theology.* Eugene, OR: Cascade, 2017.

Jacobsen, David Schnasa, and Robert A. Kelly. *Kairos Preaching: Speaking Gospel to the Situation.* Minneapolis: Fortress, 2009.

Jones, Serene. *Feminist Theory and Christian Theology: Cartographies of Grace; Guides to Theological Inquiry.* Minneapolis: Fortress, 2000.

———. *Trauma and Grace: Theology in a Ruptured World.* Louisville, KY: Westminster John Knox, 2009.

Kamkar, Katy. "Moral Injury." *CAMH*, September 14, 2017. https://www.camh.ca/en/camh-news-and-stories/moral-injury.

Keshgegian, Flora A. *Redeeming Memories: A Theology of Healing and Transformation.* Nashville: Abingdon, 2000.

Kirmayer, Laurence J., et al., eds. *Understanding Trauma: Integrating Biological, Clinical, and Cultural Perspectives.* Cambridge: Cambridge University Press, 2007.

Levi, Primo. *Survival in Auschwitz.* Translated by Stuart Woolf. New York: Macmillan, 1961.

Lewis, Alan E. *Between Cross and Resurrection: A Theology of Holy Saturday.* Grand Rapids: Eerdmans, 2001.

Lifton, Robert Jay. "Concept of the Survivor." In *Home from the War: Vietnam Veterans: Neither Victims nor Executioners.* New York: Simon & Schuster, 1973.

Long, Thomas G. *The Witness of Preaching.* 2nd ed. Louisville, KY: Westminster John Knox, 2005.

———. *What Shall We Say? Evil, Suffering, and the Crisis of Faith*. Grand Rapids: Eerdmans, 2011.

March for Our Lives. "Mission & Story." https://marchforourlives.com/mission-story/.

Mays, James. *Psalms*. Interpretation: A Bible Commentary for Teaching and Preaching. Louisville, KY: Westminster John Knox, 1994.

McCain, Shawn. "Introducing the Sacramental Imagination." *Anglican Compass*, September 30, 2015. https://anglicanpastor.com/introducing-the-sacramental-imagination/.

McCullough, Amy P. "Her Preaching Body: Embodiment and the Female Preaching Body." *Practical Matters Journal*, March 1, 2013. http://practicalmattersjournal.org/2013/03/01/preaching-body/.

Merritt, Jonathan. "'Glorious Glitter Bomb': Critics Loved 'Jesus Christ Superstar,' but Much of Religious America Was Unimpressed." *The Washington Post*, April 2, 2018. https://www.washingtonpost.com/news/acts-of-faith/wp/2018/04/02/glorious-glitter-bomb-critics-loved-jesus-christ-superstar-but-much-of-religious-america-was-unimpressed/.

Morton, Nellie. *The Journey is Home*. Boston: Beacon, 1985.

O'Connor, Kathleen M. *Lamentations and the Tears of the World*. Maryknoll, NY: Orbis, 2002.

Organ, Deborah. "Speaking the Grief Inside our Bones: Preaching and Trauma." Lectures at Moreau Seminary. Notre Dame, IN: John S. Marten Program in Homiletics and Liturgics, September 22, 2016, 1:02:29. https://www.youtube.com/watch?v=rh1uvvY24-0.

Pitzele, Peter. *Scripture Windows: Toward a Practice of Bibliodrama*. Los Angeles: Torah Aura, 1998.

Poser, Ruth. "No Words: The Book of Ezekiel as Trauma Literature and a Response to Exile." Translated by D. L. Schneider. In *Bible Through the Lens of Trauma*, edited by Elizabeth Boase and Christopher G. Frechette, 27–48. Atlanta: Society of Biblical Literature, 2016.

Powery, Luke A. *Spirit Speech: Lament and Celebration in Preaching*. Nashville: Abingdon, 2009.

Rah, Soong-Chan. "The American Church's Absence of Lament." *Sojourners*, October 24, 2013. https://sojo.net/articles/12-years-slave/american-churchs-absence-lament.

———. *Prophetic Lament: A Call for Justice in Troubled Times*. Downers Grove, IL: InterVarsity, 2015.

Rambo, Shelly. *Resurrecting Wounds: Living in the Afterlife of Trauma*. Waco, TX: Baylor University Press, 2017.

———. "Spirit and Trauma." *Interpretation* 69 (2015) 7–19.

———. *Spirit and Trauma: A Theology of Remaining*. Louisville, KY: Westminster John Knox, 2010.

———. "'Theologians Engaging Trauma' Transcript" (panel discussion). *Theology Today* 68 (October 1, 2011) 224–37.

Rendon, Jim. *Upside: The New Science of Post-traumatic Growth*. New York: Touchstone, 2015.

Renk, Leony. "Where Do You Come From? Where Are You Going? Feminist Interreligious Bibliodrama in a German Context." In *Feminist Biblical Studies in the Twentieth Century: Scholarship and Movement*, edited by Elizabeth Schussler Fiorenza, 309–24. Atlanta: Society of Biblical Literature, 2014.

Resner, André. *Living In-Between: Lament, Justice, and the Persistence of the Gospel.* Eugene, OR: Wipf & Stock, 2015.

Rice, Charles. *The Embodied Word: Preaching as Art and Liturgy.* Fortress Resources for Preaching. Minneapolis: Fortress, 1991.

Rickard, Theresa. "The Preacher as Midwife." In *The Witness of Preaching,* edited by Thomas G. Long, 13. Louisville, KY: Westminster John Knox, 2005.

Rogers, Annie G. *The Unsayable: The Hidden Language of Trauma by Annie Rogers.* Repr. New York: Random, 2007.

Sancken, Joni S. "When our Words Fail Us: Preaching Gospel to Trauma Survivors." In *Theologies of the Gospel in Context: The Crux of Homiletical Theology.* Vol. 3 of *The Promise of Homiletical Theology,* edited by David S. Jacobsen, 113–37. Eugene, OR: Cascade, 2017.

———. *Words That Heal: Preaching Hope to Wounded Souls.* The Artistry in Preaching Series. Nashville: Abingdon, 2019.

Saulny, Susan. "A Legacy of the Storm: Depression and Suicide." *The New York Times,* June 21, 2006. https://www.nytimes.com/2006/06/21/us/21depress.html.

Schüssler Fiorenza, Elisabeth, ed. *Feminist Biblical Studies in the Twentieth Century: Scholarship and Movement.* The Bible and Women: An Encyclopedia of Exegesis and Cultural History 9.1. Atlanta: Society of Biblical Literature, 2014.

Smith, Eric. "How to Be a Midwife in Egypt: A Sermon on Ferguson and Our Choices." *Faith Forward,* August 25, 2014. https://www.patheos.com/blogs/faithforward/2014/08/how-to-be-a-midwife-in-egypt-a-sermon-on-ferguson-and-our-choices/.

Stewart, Jan, and Dania El Chaar. "Syrian Youth: A Focus on Settlement, Education, and Mental Health." November 2017. http://p2pcanada.ca/wp-content/blogs.dir/1/files/2017/11/A2-Jan-Stewart.pdf.

Swinton, John. *Raging with Compassion: Pastoral Responses to the Problem of Evil.* Grand Rapids: Eerdmans, 2007.

Taylor, Barbara Brown. *The Preaching Life.* Cambridge, MA: Cowley, 1993.

Terr, L. C. "Chowchilla Revisited: The Effects of Psychic Trauma Four Years After a School-Bus Kidnapping." *American Journal of Psychiatry* 140 (1983) 1543–50.

Thomas, Tiffany. "Preaching in the Midst of Tragedy." WomenLeaders.com, June 15, 2016. https://www.christianitytoday.com/women-leaders/2016/june/preaching-in-midst-of-tragedy.html.

Tietje, Adam D. *Toward a Pastoral Theology of Holy Saturday: Providing Spiritual Care for War Wounded Souls.* Eugene, OR: Wipf & Stock, 2018.

Travis, Sarah. *Decolonizing Preaching: The Pulpit as Postcolonial Space.* Eugene, OR: Cascade, 2014.

———. "Sermon, Advent 3." Advent, 2017. presbyterian.ca/wp-content/uploads/Advent-3-sermon.pdf.

Troeger, Thomas H. "Imagination/Creativity." In *The New Interpreters Handbook of Preaching,* edited by Paul Scott Wilson, 191–92. Nashville: Abingdon, 2008.

———. "Solid Meanings Unfold: The Terror of Resurrection." *Lexington Theological Quarterly* 36 (2001) 69.

The Truth and Reconciliation Commission of Canada. *The Survivors Speak: A Report of the Truth and Reconciliation Commission of Canada,* 2015. http://www.trc.ca/assets/pdf/Survivors_Speak_English_Web.pdf.

United States Holocaust Memorial Museum. "Elie Wiesel: Elie Wiesel's Remarks at the Dedication Ceremonies for the United States Holocaust Memorial Museum, April 22, 1993." https://www.ushmm.org/information/about-the-museum/mission-and-history/wiesel.

University of Colorado Boulder. "Batman Origin Story: Original Text." August 5, 2016. https://www.colorado.edu/academics/pop-culture-and-your-intellectual-journey/batman-origin-story-original-text.

Van der Kolk, Bessel. *The Body Keeps the Score: Brain, Mind, and Body in the Healing of Trauma*. New York: Viking, 2014.

Volf, Miroslav. *Exclusion and Embrace: A Theological Exploration of Identity, Otherness, and Reconciliation*. Nashville: Abingdon, 1996.

Weingarten, Kathy. *Common Shock: Witnessing Violence Every Day; How We Are Harmed and How We Can Heal*. New York: Dutton, 2003.

Westermann, Claus. "The Role of the Lament in the Theology of the Old Testament." *Interpretation* 28 (1974) 20–38.

"What Is Bibliodrama?" Bibliodrama.com. http://www.bibliodrama.com/what-is-bibliodrama/.

"What Is Developmental Trauma / ACEs?" Portico. https://www.porticonetwork.ca/web/childhood-trauma-toolkit/developmental-trauma/what-is-developmental-trauma.

Wilson, Paul Scott. *The Four Pages of the Sermon: A Guide to Biblical Preaching*. Nashville: Abingdon, 2018.

———. *Preaching and Homiletical Theory*. Preaching and Its Partners. St. Louis: Chalice, 2004.

———, ed. *The New Interpreter's Handbook of Preaching*. Nashville: Abingdon, 2008.

Yansen, James W. S. *Daughter Zion's Trauma: A Trauma Informed Reading of Lamentations*. Piscataway, NJ: Gorgias, 2019.

.

Printed in Great Britain
by Amazon

29724905R00081